R E M E M B E R I N G
HIGHLANDS

REMEMBERING

HIGHLANDS

FROM PIONEER VILLAGE TO MOUNTAIN RETREAT

ISABEL HALL CHAMBERS
& OVERTON CHAMBERS

THE
History
PRESS

Published by The History Press
Charleston, SC 29403
www.historypress.net

Front cover, top image, courtesy of R. Henry Scadin and the Highlands Historical Society.

First published 2009

Manufactured in the United States

ISBN 978.1.59629.791.3

Library of Congress Cataloging-in-Publication Data

Chambers, Isabel Hall.
Remembering Highlands : from pioneer village to mountain retreat / Isabel Hall
Chambers and Overton Chambers.
p. cm.
Includes bibliographical references and index.
ISBN 978-1-59629-791-3 (alk. paper)
1. Highlands (N.C.)--History. 2. Highlands (N.C.--Social life and customs. 3. Highlands
(N.C.)--Biography. I. Chambers, Overton. II. Title.
F264.H63C53 2009
975.6'982--dc22
2009030567

We would like to dedicate this book to our three sons: Overton Tucker Chambers, Thomas Tudor Chambers and Timothy Gilbert Chambers, whose family history is a part of their lives.

Let us Preserve the Past,
While we Protect the Present,
So that we may have a Future.

—Anonymous

CONTENTS

CONTENTS

Part III. History and Other Interesting Vignettes of Highlands

Part IV. Family

ACKNOWLEDGEMENTS

We would like to thank, first and foremost, Janet Cummings and Marjorie Fielding, the Laurel Girls. Back in the spring of 2002, they came to ask Isabel if she would write a history article on Highlands for their new full-color magazine, the *Mountain Laurel*. Isabel said she would if Tony would type it. As a wannabe writer, Tony agreed. We missed the second issue but made all of the deadlines after that.

Janet and Marjorie and Guy Fielding have been kind enough to help us with photographs and suggestions that they have received from their readers. We both feel fortunate to have been asked to do this and appreciate more than words can express our chance to bring back some of the "good old times and places." They also offered their professional expertise to put all the stories and photographs in the right media and format for the publisher.

We thank MaryAnn Sloan, our friend and assistant librarian, for proofing this. We have learned to have a third party work to find the obvious and not-so-obvious flaws.

Also special thanks to Dr. Randolph Shaffner and his book, *Heart of the Blue Ridge: Highland, North Carolina* His thorough and definitive history of Highlands was a great help when we got stuck. In addition, he helped us in the pre-publication phase of this work.

Laura All, our commissioning editor, gave us good advice and encouragement from the start to see this through to publication.

Finally, we thank all the folks that told us their stories, as well as gave firsthand information of the people and events that they knew.

INTRODUCTION

There's a village on the Highlands Plateau that was not started like the other towns and villages in Western North Carolina. It was not a place that one or more pioneer families, moving west from the coast or down the Appalachians, decided to settle. Instead, two entrepreneur developers conceived Highlands on a map as the future center of trade in the East. They did this from as far away as Hutchinson, Kansas, a town that Clinton Carter Hutchinson and Samuel Truman Kelsey had founded.

The two men struggled up to the top of the plateau, where they found only a few buildings in the area. There were small settlements in the coves and valleys surrounding the plateau that had been settled years before by Scotch-Irish, Germans and English coming from the east, up from the south and, earlier, down the Appalachians from Pennsylvania.

Kelsey and Hutchinson represented a kind of early developer. They were here to create a town and make money from land sales. Kelsey printed a pamphlet that was sent all over the United States proclaiming the healthy climate and excellent place for the fruit grower, farmer and stock grower. The pamphlet reached as far away as the Midwest and the New England states. Soon single men and women and whole families began arriving from places like Wisconsin, Connecticut and New Hampshire. They were people of substance and professionals.

Through the early years the town struggled, and both Kelsey and Hutchinson left, but the original settlers remained and thrived. Schools were established, churches were built and, later, culture came in the form of the

Highlands Improvement Society, the Hudson Library and the Highlands Biological Association. The Hudson Library is one of the oldest public libraries in North Carolina. Along with culture, a tuberculosis sanatorium was established, which brought many patients from other parts of the country for the cure.

Throughout the intervening years, the village has grown and prospered. As early as the 1880s, families from the South learned of the cool climate and began building summer homes in which to vacation during the long, hot and humid summer months. About 1900, the first golf courses were built. When automobiles became popular, the journey to Highlands from as far away as New Orleans became practical. Improvement in public services such as electricity, water, sewer and telephones attracted more summer visitors, and gradually hotels were offering seasonal rates to those who couldn't afford to buy or build a home. So Highlands grew, not as a trading center but as a resort.

In the past half century, the village's year-round population doubled from five hundred to almost one thousand. Not a great number, but when the surrounding areas are added and the summer residents and visitors are included, the number increases to over twenty thousand. A state-of-the-art hospital, a nursing home, a retirement village, the Martin-Lipscomb Performing Arts Center, the Bascom Center for the Visual Arts, a modern library and multiple playhouses are just a sampling of what draws visitors and new residents to our village.

All of this has led to an interest in the past, the history of Highlands and those who made it. Less than ten years ago, a small group of history-minded citizens began to retrieve the past within photos, family histories, diaries and, yes, permanent homes. The group, formally named the Highlands Historical Society, Inc., along with other interested individuals, purchased the oldest home in Highlands. The Prince House, as it is familiarly called, was built in 1877 and is located within walking distance of Main Street on the Cashiers Road. With acquisition of the old Hudson Library building, which was moved to the Prince House location, the property is now known as Highlands Historic Village. The old library building is now the repository of written and photographic records, as well as the museum for artifacts. History buffs and those looking for their roots in Highlands are welcome to do research.

As you read through the book, you will discover not only stories of our early pioneers but also insight into what life was like from the early

1900s to the 1940s—courtesy of one of our authors and our storyteller. Some of our stories have narratives that we have based on the bare facts of those involved.

In addition to personal and family stories, we have gathered short biographies of interesting persons whose history begins or ends in Highlands. We hope you will enjoy your travels through these stories.

PART I

MEMORIES OF DAYS GONE BY

H ere is a collection of stories that go back as far as the mid-1930s. Some are humorous, some informative and some relate just how it was back when Highlands was like any other small town.

ICE SKATING IN HIGHLANDS

We don't know if the American Indians tried ice skating; probably not. However, ice skating on Highlands' lakes goes back almost one hundred years. We know that there was skating on Mirror Lake, formerly Stewart's Pond, in the 1920s. Margaret Hall remembers this when her parents had a home on Cullasaja Drive on the upper end of the lake, and this was before the "Big Lake," Lake Sequoyah, was created. There was also skating on the lake at the Hall House golf links after 1900. Back then we think they used skates that strapped onto boots. One of the hazards skaters encountered in those early days were holes left in the ice after ice blocks were cut out to store in the icehouses around town. The Hall House had such a building. Stored properly with sawdust as insulation, the ice would keep into the summer.

Skating back then was a lot like we can remember, but the ice was thicker and it was mostly local residents that enjoyed the activity. Even then there was evening skating on moonlit nights. Folks would drive from town, or walk, bringing their own skates and maybe something to sit on. There was plenty of downed wood to build a fire and roast marshmallows, and one

Ice skating on Lake Sequoyah—Tom Harbison and his two daughters.

could watch the skaters or take a break from skating. There were docks on the lake back then, and they served as another resting spot. At that time, it was possible to skate up the lake all the way to Pinkerton's pool, where the Cullasaja River goes under Cashiers Road.

In the late 1920s, the dam was built to make Lake Sequoyah, and this gave the skaters a much larger place to test their skills. It was not unusual to have cars drive onto the ice on Sequoyah, either. Larger groups could play crack the whip on skates. This was a favorite game for the younger generation. About this time, when the word got out about ice on our lakes, we got a large crowd from upper South Carolina. Folks from Anderson, Pickens and Greenville would drive up for the day, and that started a skate rental business. I believe Carter Talley was the first to offer this service; later, Steve Potts also rented skates.

One of the better-known skaters was Jim "GI" Hines. He had long racing skates and could do just as well backward as forward. There weren't many to challenge Jim in a race.

Harris Lake was another place that skaters liked. Although smaller than the other two lakes, it was right in town and kids could go after school without having to go to the larger lakes. Much later, the town would string lights so there could be skating at night, moon or no moon.

Back in January 1956, the *Atlanta Journal* ran an article on skating in Highlands in their Sunday magazine section. It reminded us of a lot of folks who aren't here anymore, but it was a well-written piece. Nowadays, we don't get very many good days of skating ice. Some say that it's due to putting salt on the roads in the winter, others say landing on the moon did it. But if you want to find out if there is good skating ice in the winter, give the Highlands Chamber of Commerce a call.

COW SITTING AND THE TOWN BALL

Back in the first half of the last century, there were a number of fields around town, and there were as many cows as there were fields. Some folks had a cow but no field, and some had a field but no cow. Along Fifth Street there were several fields where the old Hall House Golf Links had been. If you had a cow but no field of your own, you could take your cow to a neighbor's field and stake it.

During the summer when school was out, cow sitting, or pasturing as we might call it today, was usually done by the daughters of the family—just like it was done in Europe, when the cows would be taken up to the high meadows in the summer. The cow would be led down the street to a field and staked out with a long rope. The cow had to be trained for this to keep it from tripping on the rope and perhaps breaking a leg. As you can imagine, this would have been a boring way to spend the day. You didn't have fences unless you had a cow and a field of your own.

Enter the game of town ball. Only girls played our version usually, but occasionally boys would be allowed. Other girls in the neighborhood would join the girls keeping the cows. Just as in baseball today, there was home plate and first, second and third base. If nothing else was available for the bases, dried cow pies or meadow muffins were used. Sometimes there were regular baseball bats and softballs, but if these weren't available, and usually they weren't, a tennis ball and a flat bat were the usual equipment. A flat bat was just a short board, perhaps a one by four that had been whittled down on one end, with the flat part hopefully hitting the ball. Choosing up sides was always a painful experience for the younger, smaller girls. Since there weren't many girls to choose from, the team captains would have to finally pick the small ones.

An old field on Fifth Street, formerly part of the Hall House Golf Course.

There may not have been more than two or three on each team, so throwing the ball and hitting the runner was as good as tagging her out. Just like today, a caught fly was also an out. Once out, a player would have to score three runs to get back in the game. This was done by running for the batter when she had a hit. Some of the players were better runners than hitters. Hitting a cow with the ball would count as an out. Another automatic out would be hitting the ball into a neighbors' vegetable garden. If the player was not careful retrieving the ball and damaged some corn or tomato plants, she would be out of the game. During the game, the cow would be moved to fresh grass, and so the playing field would also move. And one always had to watch out for cow pies.

Boys usually played by different rules, and they didn't have to deal with a cow. In our neighborhood, the Crisp girls had the cow, and other girls, including some Pottses and Halls would be the regulars. The girls handled this whole game without any help from parents, coaches or refreshment stands.

We came across an interesting note recently that town ball was played in Savannah, Georgia, back in the 1830s much like we have described the game here.

Memories of Days Gone By

ONE RINGY DINGY, TWO RINGY DINGY

Lily Tomlin performed a caricature act of a telephone operator from times gone by on *Saturday Night Live*. We would like to take you back to those days in Highlands, when the switchboard connected us with the outside world. My grandmother, Meta Norton Frost Hall, operated the Highlands Telephone Company in the early 1920s. Three daughters, Mattie, Caroline and Dorothy, and two sons, Jack and Tudor, were employees at one time or another. Jack and Tudor strung wire, maintained the system and installed the phones. Mattie, Dorothy and later Caroline and others were the operators. Back at the start, there weren't many homes with phones; usually businesses and only the very well-to-do could afford to have the service.

According to Ran Shaffner in his book *Heart of the Blue Ridge: Highlands, North Carolina*, Captain Prioleau Ravenel brought the first telephone service to Highlands from Horse Cove and on to Cashiers in 1901. Later on, Dr. Mary Lapham had the telephone franchise. But it was in the early '20s that the Halls leased the system.

Back then there were fewer than one hundred phones, and so your number was only two digits. Some old-timers can still remember their numbers. Isabel's was 25. In 1929, Western Carolina Telephone Company took over the system, but local operators still ran the switchboard. The office was first located on the second floor of the Holt building at the corner of Fourth and Main Streets. The on-duty operator could just look out the window to see up and down the street. It was not unusual for someone to place a call and be told that their party wasn't home as he or she was out in front of one of the stores or that they had gone to Franklin for the day and wouldn't be home until late. The operators knew most everything that went on in town.

Two- and four-party lines were the norm. Donald Davis, a nationally known storyteller who grew up in Western North Carolina, has a great yarn about a man just getting a phone for the first time. He was on a four-party line and could never get through because of two elderly ladies that spent the day chatting to each other. Finally, when he did get through, he called a friend and related to the friend that there was a great flood coming through and that he should hang his phone out the window so the water coming through the lines would not flood the house. He later drove past one of the ladies' homes and noticed that her phone was hanging out the window.

In the Highlands telephone office, there was a cot either in the room with the switchboard or next to it. The night operator used this. Through the years, many familiar names come to mind as operators: Manila Reese, Elizabeth Newton and Ethel Calloway, to name a few. There was a line out the Buck Creek Road, mainly for the U.S. Forest Service, but early on others were added to it. Later, the office was moved to part of what was the building housing the Christmas Tree on the Hill, but now that building too is gone. It was right at sidewalk level, so passersby would stop and chat with the operator. I can remember calling Isabel long distance, and after several calls I memorized the routing codes used by Ma Bell. Then when I placed the call I gave the operator the codes and it went through a lot faster.

During World War II, there were still some homes without phones. Sons, husbands and boyfriends would call the nearest neighbor that had a phone to get a message to their family or loved one. If the neighbor lived close enough, many times a young child would be sent running to the family. Many of these young children still remember those dashes to a neighbor's house and how exciting it was.

General Telephone & Electronics (GTE) took over Western Carolina Telephone Company in the '60s or '70s. By then, the office had been moved out of Highlands to Sylva. There was still a human voice to talk to, though. Burnett Cagle had a TV repair shop in town. His wife, Dolly, was a long-distance operator in Sylva. It wasn't unusual to call information and Dolly would answer, recognize your voice and ask, "Tony, is that you?" Then we would have a short chat and would catch up on each other's family.

Nowadays, you're lucky to talk to a human voice. I tried once to call about a mistake on my phone bill and never could get anything but a computer voice. Finally I had to write a letter. Wouldn't you think that the business that made its money from transmitting the human voice would make a better effort to communicate with its customers?

The days of a local phone service and local customer service are long gone. Perhaps we couldn't live with the old system now, but you'll probably agree that it certainly was friendlier.

THE OLD SCHOOLHOUSE

The old bell that used to ring out from on top of the old Highlands School has a new home atop our town hall. But there are a number of Highlanders who attended the school before the 1950s and remember the school and its surroundings.

Recently, the steps that led from Highway 64, Cashiers Road, up to the school have been uncovered. You can view those that remain that lead from the parking area in back of the town hall up to the parking area at the ABC store. Back in 1930s and '40s, many children walked up from the Cashiers roadside, including the Henrys, Becks, Halls, Thompsons, McDowells, Pottses , Gibsons, Edwardses and many more. Another contingent including the Andersons, Cobbs, Cooks, Wallers and Creswells came up from Main Street, between Fred Edwards's store (now the Ann Jacob Gallery) and Potts Brothers Market (now Dutchman's Design). The path went through the empty lot that is now Cyrano's bookstore. That path ran up to Oak Street and then up rougher steps to the front of the school. Buses brought children from Flat Mountain, Clear Creek, Horse Cove, Scaly Mountain, Turtle Pond and Shortoff after the one-room schools there were consolidated with Highlands School. The buses came up Oak Street and let off the children at the top of the hill beside the school.

When you got to school early, as many did, particularly those who arrived by bus, the girls and boys separated and gathered at the top on one side of the steps according to gender. There were tall hedges on either side, and

The old Highlands School.

different groups would gather according to their age. Many of the younger boys, up to preteens, would be found on their knees shooting marbles or playing mumbely peg. On the other side of the steps, the younger girls would be jumping rope to the time-honored cadences of "Miss Lucy," "Doctor Doctor," "Miss Polly had a Dolly" or "I Met a Girl Named Sally." When the inside bell rang, everyone would stop their play and go inside for class.

During recess, the groups changed as each class had its own area between different hedges. They played group games including blindman's bluff, red rover, hide-and-seek, snake in the gulley, kick the can, drop the handkerchief, Old MacDonald and in and out the window. The older boys and girls went down to the area now used for parking in the back of the school, where there was a basketball court of sorts.

We think the hedges were the idea of Henry Worrell Sloan. Mr. Sloan built his home on Satulah Mountain at the beginning of the last century and had formal gardens with similar hedges. He was very interested in our school. He arranged the first movies to be shown in Highlands in the school lunchroom. Later on, a separate auditorium building was built by the Works Progress Administration (WPA) and now houses the Highlands Playhouse. The first movies were silent films. Mr. Sloan possibly bought the piano, but we are sure he bought the Pianola that pulled up to the upright piano and played from paper rolls like other player pianos. The Pianola was still located in the Sloan house when it was sold and the contents auctioned off.

The primary-grade classrooms were located on the first floor, and the high school classrooms were on the second floor along with the one room that included the kitchen and lunchroom. In the winter, the janitor would go from room to room, filling the potbellied stoves with coal. By the time he had made his rounds, it was time to start over. Snow days were rare, but if the water pipes froze the school was closed for the day.

Several of the high school boys would play indoor hooky. They would climb up to the attic and do what older boys do. At least once, the game was up when one fell through the second-floor ceiling.

The school fielded its first basketball teams in 1948, both a boys' team and a girls' team. They played on a clay court with no roof or walls.

After the new school was finished at the end of South Fifth Street, the town used the old school as a sort of recreation center. A shuffleboard court was painted in one of the hallways. That was tough to do as the floors had been oiled for years, and paint didn't want to stick. Where the basketball court used to be, they made a clay tennis court—our summer rains made keeping that court smooth and flat a real job. Some of the directors of the center were Reverend Robert "Bob" B. DuPree, Richard B. "Snook" Thompson and Overton "Tony" Chambers. These same men were in charge of the annual Hillbilly Day celebrations in the early 1950s.

Well, all of that is gone now, except for the stone steps and those young children who are now senior citizens and would be glad to tell you their stories. Our dream would be to have a bronze statue of children playing where they used to play—forever young. If you share that dream give us a call or send a letter.

AROUND OUR BLOCK

Sarah, Isabel and Buddy Hall.

I'd like to tell you about the block where I grew up. At one time, the entire block belonged to my grandparents. They sold off several parts, but the rest was like a country club. My parents built our home on the property in the early 1930s. Back then, there still existed many of the features of a club, including the hotel, guesthouses, lake, clay tennis court and parts of the nine-hole golf course.

My grandmother divided much of the property between her seven children before she sold the hotel. That's where my family comes in. We had the tennis court and one of the golf greens on our lot. We also had some of the golf clubs from both of our left-handed grandfathers. My sister, brother and I played golf on our one green with those clubs and used black walnuts for balls. Our putting wasn't very good, but boy could we smack those walnuts. Our mother didn't appreciate the walnut shells all over the yard.

Then we had the tennis court. On Sundays, the adults would gather at the court and play mixed foursomes. That was after church and Sunday dinner. All of my aunts and uncles lived in Highlands except for Aunt Deas, who was married to Judge Broyles from Atlanta, and Uncle Harry, who would come to visit in the summer. Aunt Dosie, who was married to Roy Potts, and Aunt Caroline kept the hotel open in the summer. Aunt Mattie was married to Uncle Charlie Anderson; Uncle Jack was married to Sue Rucker. Well, they all had a good time, and we played around the sidelines. There were nine of us cousins, and we got along pretty well most of the time.

The lot next to ours was Uncle Jack and Aunt Sue's. They built a house but later moved to Decatur when the war started. In fact, they were the only other brother or sister besides my parents who built on the property. And next to theirs was Uncle Harry's lot, and now that belongs to the Harris family. The big boys, as we called them, would play football on Uncle Harry's lot. It was nice and flat and had no trees.

The next lot down was sold to Clarissa Ravenel and given to the First Presbyterian Church a long time ago. The original manse and the newer manse, where Reverend Hunter and Trudie Coleman lived, are located on that lot.

My Aunt Dosie's lot is next. In the winter, we used to sled from the Presbyterian lot across Aunt Dosie's lot. Now it belongs to Neville and Edna Bryson. Those Bryson boys were terrors on our street when they were growing up.

As for us children, sometimes we would walk over to the lake and follow the stream, Mill Creek, down to where the trailer park and recreational vehicle parks are now. Later on, Cy Stannard had a riding stable, and my sister Sarah used to go down and exercise the horses. That lot belonged to Aunt Deas. Some time ago, Ed Broyles, who lives in Franklin, talked about a picture of his great-great-uncle playing on a tennis court in Highlands. I told him that it was at the Hall House court and that he was playing with his wife, my Aunt Deas. Her lot was full of small white pines, and Indians were behind every one of them. We would spend all afternoon on some days running them off with our cap pistols.

Those lots were really deep. Out on Main Street, at the corner of Sixth Street, was Aunt Mattie's lot. That's where the Highlands Townsite Apartments are now.

Those were the days. Highlands has really changed since then. My aunts and uncles are gone. My sister, one brother and one cousin are gone. I have no one to chase the Indians with any more.

PRESBYTERIAN VACATION BIBLE SCHOOL: A HIGHLANDS STORY

Storytelling is ageless. Our oral history is based on storytelling. Without storytelling, the myths and legends wouldn't exist, and the very fabric of our civilization would be a blank page.

Memories of Days Gone By

Storytellers have always been in demand. The traveling tinkers of old were great storytellers, passing on information from one area to another, as well as adlibbing to make it more interesting. The bards of the wealthy were part of a king or a chief's retinue or tail. With that said, Isabel would like to tell you a story she presented at the Hudson Library several years ago.

When Virginia Worley asked me to tell a story tonight, I was scared to death. I was even more scared when I learned that Father Mike Jones, Buck Trott and Walter Wilson were going to tell stories, too. So I decided to tell one I have told to many of my friends, relations and those involved who don't remember.

I would like to dedicate this story to Donald Davis from Duck, North Carolina, and formally from Haywood County—a nationally known storyteller who shared the same Asheville dentist with me years ago. And he tells a great story about that, too.

The summer I was seven (I'm not telling what year that was), we lived on Fifth Street. Our family consisted of my mother and father, Margaret and Tudor Hall; my grandmother, Bessie Gilbert; Sarah; and my younger brother, Buddy. Sarah was taller, prettier, smarter and definitely someone I should look up to.

My mother had been talking to her neighbor, the Presbyterian minister, and heard his church would be having Vacation Bible School starting Monday. Well, what do you think mother told us? "You and Sarah should go." At that time, our Episcopal church had only three children: Sarah, Buddy and me. Mother was told we would be welcome if we went. Remember that!

When Monday morning rolled around, no matter how we objected and protested that we did not want to go, mother said we were going. Sarah decided how we should dress (as she always knew best). So we put on our little calico dresses with puffed sleeves, a wide pink-white sash in the back, black patent leather shoes, "Mary Janes," and white socks. We were all ready except for our hair. Sarah had very fine, straight hair. She yelled a lot when mother combed it. My hair was a little better; I never screamed or yelled. Only big sisters get away with that. I just let Grandmother tie part of it up with a big bow.

Now, like it or not, we were ready. The plan was to cross the street and meet Sarah's friend, Anne Patrick Major, who lived in the big Sullivan house. We were given the rules. Walk straight to the church and straight back after it was over at noon.

Crossing Fifth Street was a snap, as it was just a one-lane-wide, dusty dirt road with no traffic. Then we walked up a set of steps about five feet wide

The Presbyterian church.

with cement blocks cast to look like stone. At the bottom of the steps were wood posts on each side. Sarah told me they were hitching posts for horses.

Anyway, we climbed the stairs to the sidewalk, which was a dirt path about three feet wide. There was a wall, made of the same blocks that ran down to the corner, which supported the sidewalk. A white picket fence surrounded the house, and behind it there was a forest of hemlock, white pine, balsam, rhododendron and laurel. You couldn't see the house from the fence. Sarah opened the white picket gate, where there was a paved walk to the house. We walked through a tunnel of trees that smelled like Christmas. At the end of the walk was a row of boxwoods in front of the porch. Up on the porch were big rocking chairs, and in one was a little old lady with gold-rimmed glasses and long black and gray hair pinned, tucked and netted in place—in case the wind from rocking might blow it away. She was dressed all in black: black dress, black shoes and black stockings. As she rocked, her feet didn't touch the floor since she was so short. Only when she came forward and pushed did her feet touch. She looked up and smiled and called out, "Anne Patrick." And out Anne Patrick bounced like a jack-in-the-box. She must have been waiting behind the front door. Anne was taller than me, because she was so much older.

We said goodbye to "Maa-Maa" and ran down the walk to the sidewalk. Then we turned right to follow the white picket fence to the corner at Pine Street. Sarah picked up a stick and so did I. Sarah began running it along the fence—*click-clunk, click-clunk*. We made a great sound, but Anne Patrick said Maa-Maa didn't like us to do that. I dropped my stick, but Sarah kept right on *click-clunk, click-clunk*. It didn't matter, though, as we were at the corner of Pine Street.

If we had turned the corner, we would have followed the white picket fence down to the Cashiers Road. About where the gazebo is now, inside the fence there was a wishing well (really a springhouse) covered with a shed very much like the present gazebo but in Adirondack style. It was covered with little twigs and had a split-oak shingle roof. There wasn't any floor but stones stairs that led down to the well. When we played in the Sullivan yard, we would walk down to the stone stairs for a drink of water. We used a folded rhododendron leaf for a cup.

Sometimes we didn't get a drink because there were either little orange salamanders or black ones or even a big black one with red spots. Though Sarah said it was good water if "lizards" lived in it, I still wouldn't drink any.

If we had gone farther, we would have come to two large flowerbeds inside the fence. They were raised about a foot and were about ten by twelve feet. One was full of beautiful purple heather and the other with white heather. I wish they were still there. (I learned many years later that Dr. Anderson, who built the house, had married a woman from Scotland and that she was responsible for the heather.)

If we had gone all the way to the corner at the Cashiers Road, which was as far as we were allowed to go, we would have watched the garage across the street. There was a tall, handsome, blue-eyed man there named Richard Zoellner, who worked for his father, Carl. Richard had met the young woman who worked for my family named Ella Mae Keener. We were determined that Richard should marry her. He had other girls that would go to see him. One, whom we called the "Blonde Blizzard," would ride up on her brown Tennessee walking horse. Sarah said that's the kind of horse it was. Anyway, when she came and tied her horse up to the fence, we would hide so she never knew we were there. But we couldn't see or hear what they said because of the horse. Then we ran back to our house to see if Ella Mae Keener was there, to tell her. And she told us to run back and try to listen. By then, the "Blonde Blizzard" would be gone. She got a ticket once for riding on the sidewalk.

Then there was Virginia, a dark-haired girl from Florida. She liked Richard, too. One day she had a meeting in our front yard with Ella Mae. I don't know why. I was the runner who went to "our corner," across from the garage, and told Richard about it. Ella Mae and Richard did get married later on, and we take full credit for it. She and some of their children still live in Highlands.

But I've gotten sidetracked again. One story does lead to another. Well that day, Monday, we had to go straight to the Presbyterian church. We couldn't turn at the corner of Pine. At that corner, there were more stone steps leading from the sidewalk to the street. They were higher than the steps leading up from Fifth Street to the Sullivan house. At the bottom of the steps were two more hitching posts. Then there was a ditch at the bottom of the steps. We climbed out of that and crossed Pine Street—only back then we didn't know it had a name. We went to the vacant lot on the other side, where there was a rusty old steam tractor parked. It had been there ever since its first and last trip to Seneca to pick up mail and supplies for Highlands. A group of Highlands businessmen had formed a company, the Highlands Traction Company, and bought the tractor. I understand it didn't work out, but that's another story. We made many a trip on the old rusty seat, two of us riding shotgun as we made imaginary trips down to Moccasin, Georgia. We jumped off because we knew we were going to be late.

We passed the old John Jay Smith House on our right. We didn't go close. Everyone knew it was haunted. And that's another story. Finally, we got to Main Street and saw the Presbyterian church looming up ahead on the hill. We crossed dusty Main Street and came to the steps that used to come all the way down to the street. At the top of the first set of steps was the fence and gate that you see today. Still we didn't want to go up the second set of steps, but we were afraid mother would do something if we didn't. But we were stopped at the gate by three of our Anderson cousins: Totsie, Anne and Mary Deas Anderson. We called them "Flopsie," "Mopsie" and "Cotton Tail."

They said all together, "You can't come in. You don't belong. You go back across the street where you do belong."

Try as we might, we couldn't get in. They even got more help from the other Presbyterian children. But we didn't care. Didn't want to go anyway. So we turned and went back down the street steps and headed home. This time we crossed to our side of the street on the Episcopal church corner, and we got our shoes and socks really dirty. On that side of the street, the hill was steeper. But it wasn't too steep if we walked in the ditches. Sometimes we would find real white clay that was slimy. On that day, we found some, and Sarah rolled it into a ball and punched the inside to form an Indian bowl. Sarah said we would have to cook it to make it hard. So off we went home, each of us carrying a handful of clay.

As we walked toward our front door, we met mother. She was tall with dark, curly hair and very pretty. With her finger pointing at us she said, "What do you all think you are doing back here?"

Sarah said, "We're going to make Indian bowls in the oven."

Mother's voice rose much louder, and her finger really shook at us. "What about Bible School?"

Sarah explained that they wouldn't let us in. "Don't be ridiculous," Mother said. "Get yourselves back down there. They can't keep you out."

So we put our bowls in the sun to cook and started our trek back down the road. We tried to decide what to do as we walked. We could try to go to the back gate, but they would just run around and stop us. Sarah said we could get a handful of rocks and chunk them on the head. Didn't I say my sister was smarter? But Anne didn't think that was a good idea.

As we were passing the haunted Smith House again, Sarah saw big clumps of cut grass. She said we could use it. Cut grass is very sharp. Anne and I asked how we could get it. Sarah reached in her dress pocket and pulled out a small knife. She opened it and cut each of us a handful of long leaves of cut grass, and off we went, armed now. Across the street, up the steps in single file, we marched to the church gate, me last.

Flopsie, Mopsie and Cotton Tail plus anyone else they had been able to collect were standing there with the gate closed, saying, "We said you can't come in. It's our church, not yours." So we drove them away from the gate swinging our cut grass at them. We really got their little bare legs. They began to scream, like little girls do, and ran from the gate. So in we went, driving them up the steps into the church. What with all the commotion we had caused, suddenly the maddest woman I have ever seen was standing with her hands on her hips in front of us. She was dressed in what was called a housedress, her stockings so wrinkled I thought they might fall down; her hair was black and looked like it had been ironed and put on her head. She opened her mouth to speak, and I knew we'd had it. I jumped behind Sarah and Anne.

"I don't want any trouble from you all from across the street."

I guess I have been trouble ever since.

This past July I went to the "Kirkin" of the Tartan at the Presbyterian Church. When I looked around to see whom I might sit with, I saw my cousin, Anne Anderson Sellers—Mopsie. As I sat down next to her, she whispered. "Who let you in?" and smiled.

MAIN STREET: A HIGHLANDS SUMMER, 1943

Downtown Highlands has changed mightily over the last one hundred years. We would like to take you back to when Main Street was still the hub of commerce—back when you couldn't walk more than two or three steps without greeting someone you knew. So let's travel back to that time: 1943.

It's eleven o'clock, and a number of people are gathered around the new U.S. Post Office. It is the two-story brick building that Fred Edwards had built, conveniently located in the center of Main between Fourth and Third Streets. There are lots of cars parked in front. It's the busiest time of day. With gas rationing now in full swing, most people limit their driving to only the most important tasks. All of the cars were built before 1942, and some are a lot older than that. There is a black Ford Depot hack from the mid-1930s, but its black fenders and hood shine like they had been waxed that morning, and the wood body is in excellent condition. The driver, in chauffeurs' black cap and jacket, is standing in front of the car holding a canvas and leather bag with the official "U.S. Post Office" stenciled on the front. It might be Mr. Townsend or Mr. Bliss's man. Everyone is waiting for the mail to be "put up." Gene Mays passed by earlier, bringing the Railway Express from Walhalla, South Carolina. Many older men and women are waiting for some letter from a son in the war. Vmail letters were the standard wartime stationery from overseas in the Pacific or Atlantic theatres. They were an all-in-one letter, and the envelope is made with the thinnest paper. Many times half of the letter is censored out.

There's Colonel Mobray and Admiral McCully chatting. And Mrs. Clarke Howell is going into Wit's End. Mrs. O.E. Young is putting several pieces of pottery in the window of her new shop. She had been a regular customer and friend of Addie Root, who has a very eclectic offering of gifts and whose shop is down on the corner across Main Street from the Potts House. You can drop by and buy some gift or have a cup of English tea. Alice Inman rents a room from the Roots and has a sweater shop. It is the only place in town to buy yarn. Many of the young women in town are knitting wool squares that will be sewn into blankets for the boys overseas. (Isabel thought she saw one like she had made on a recent visit to Scotland.)

Down a few doors, Mrs. Kenyon Zahner just came out of Sarah Gilder's store. A younger woman is carrying her baby into the store. Miss Gilder stocks a little bit of everything, but one of her important services is her scale. She has the only one in town, which helps a young mother keep up with her baby's weight, since we had no full-time doctor and no

Bill Holt's soda shop and Harry Holt's café.

hospital as yet. Sarah's other important function was as the clearinghouse for town gossip.

After the mail was put up, many of the women strolled down to Potts Brothers Grocery. Here Roy (also known as Nick), Frank and Ed Potts had the first grocery store in town that included a meat market. When Nick or Frank takes your grocery list, they or one of their clerks will gather up the order. Self-service hasn't reached Highlands. If you need any meat, you walk back to see the butcher, Nick's son Tom. He will go into the walk-in cooler and cut whatever you need from the side of beef or pork hanging there. Usually he will have ground meat and sausage already made and scoop out what you ask for. Of course, you have to have enough ration stamps for whatever groceries and meat that you buy. In the winter, old-timers would sit around the potbellied stove and discuss problems great and small. Another service provided by the store is home delivery. Yes, you can call in your order, if you have a telephone, or leave it when you were in town and have it delivered. They bring it into your kitchen. This is a big help to folks who can't drive or don't have enough gas ration coupons. Of course, like most stores in town they offer charge accounts. During the Depression, this service had hurt some businesses, but now times are better. Potts Brothers also offered a similar service to Sarah Gilder's. They have a heavy-duty scale that some of our heavier male residents use on occasion.

Next door, Colonel Robertson was leaving Fred Edwards store. His burlap sack slung over his shoulder is bulging with groceries and probably a bottle of whiskey. He doesn't look very well this summer. It is hard to believe he walks all the way from Shortoff at his age. Across the street, Bill Holt's soda shop and Harry Holt's café are doing a thriving business. Bill had great ice cream sodas and sundaes. Besides the café, Harry and his wife also run a taxi service, one of several operating in town. Floyd Lamb operated one out of Carter Talley's Sinclair station down at the corner of Third and Main, across from the Masonic Lodge.

Now there goes the Trailways bus, right on time. Twice a day it comes through Highlands, giving service to Atlanta and Asheville—another great form of public transportation besides the local taxi service. And like the taxis, it helps us get around with gas rationing and all.

Up on the hill, the Jackson County Bank would see business pick up after people had gone to the post office. Then people would walk up to "Doc" Mitchell's drugstore next to Charlie Anderson's dime store. Teenagers and those hoping to be teenagers come in to read the latest movie magazines before Doc stops them. Then they'll order a Coca-Cola or maybe a cherry coke. Another trial for Doc is their habit of pulling more straws out of the dispenser than is needed.

Farther down Main Street, toward the Dillard Road, Helen's Barn will be open tonight. Probably Mel and Dixie Keener will play along with several others. Between sets, teenagers will feed the jukebox nickels for the latest tunes: "One o'Clock Jump" or other jitterbug songs. Occasionally, Admiral McCully will pick a waltz and ask one of the mature women, sometimes Tony's mother, to join him. Next the caller will shout, "Everybody grab your partner for the next dance."

Then the building starts shaking as cloggers and buck dancers like Callie Beal take the floor. The music goes on until about 11:00 p.m. Between sets you can get a cold drink at the concession stand from Maxie Wright. Some drift outside for harder stuff, and there may be some courting going on in the parked cars.

Though this isn't a complete picture of Main Street sixty years ago, it is a few brush strokes on the canvas of our memory.

FROM ISABEL'S DIARY

This entry is dated May 5, 1945.

This was a big day for me. I was going to meet my friends at the drug store at the top of the hill [now Mirror Lake Antiques] to catch the bus at ten o'clock. We, Mary Bascom Cook, Mary Deas Anderson and Margaret McDowell, were all going to Joyce Burnette's birthday party in Scaly on the Trailways Bus from Asheville. Can you believe that? It was to be our first bus ride. Of course we were excited, we got to the drug store early, bought our tickets and had to check out the movie magazines. "Doc" Mitchell hated us reading the magazines and not buying them, so he snatched them out of our hands and put them back in the rack. So much for reading the magazines. We sat down and ordered one cherry smash and took five or six straws out of the dispenser. That always got "Doc" upset. I guess he was glad when the bus arrived.

When we heard the bus's horn, we ran out to meet it. Of course, we had to wait until the passengers from Asheville got off. Then the driver took the passengers' bags out and set them on the sidewalk, along with boxes and other packages that had been sent from Asheville. There was even a stack of new movie magazines for the drug store. Finally the driver, ticket taker, was ready for us. Or was he! All these young girls!

We dashed onto the bus. There weren't many passengers besides us, so we had our choice of seats. You would have thought none of us liked each other, as we all took a window seat and sat alone. We all giggled and kept moving around for a better seat, until the driver got back in, sat down and started the bus. Then the door shut.

Off we went heading west out of town on Hwy. 106. I started to hum "the wheels on the bus go round and round" and my friends gave me dirty looks, so I stopped. We passed Highlands Country Club, went through Buttermilk Level and stopped several times before getting to the Dilly Talley straight. We went around Big Scaly Mountain and looked out at Camp Paradise. Finally we passed the War Woman Road [now Hale Ridge Road], the Scaly Mountain Baptist Church and Cemetery, around a curve and there we were at the Scaly Mountain Post Office and Trailways Bus Station.

Joyce and Patsy Fisher were there to meet us. You'd have thought we just came home from a long trip. They joked and asked where our luggage was? Joyce lived in a big white house behind the Post Office. Her mother was the Postmaster. We went into the farmhouse and down the stairs to the basement, where the kitchen and dining room were. The table was set and there was a white birthday cake with pink candles as the centerpiece. We all sat down and tried to be lady-like (like real ladies) as Joyce's mother and older sisters waited on us. After a large lunch followed by cake and ice cream, Joyce opened the presents we had given her. I remember someone gave her a sterling silver I.D. bracelet with "Joyce" engraved on it. I gave her a "Slam Book" and each of us filled a page. Then we went upstairs to her bedroom on the top floor and looked at movie magazines and her movie star photo collection. We'd each brought some of ours and traded around. Van Johnson was one our favorites, then Roddy McDowell and Clark Gable. The pictures were all different sizes, 3x5, 5x7 and 8x10. All you had to do was send a penny postcard to the studios and ask for an autographed picture. Most of them came with a stamped signature but some had real signatures.

The day went really fast as we were having so much fun. But then Mrs. Burnett called us and said the bus had arrived from Atlanta. So we rushed downstairs, told everyone thank you, that we had a great day and got on the bus to go back to Highlands.

Can you believe that in 1945 we had buses coming through Highlands from Asheville to Atlanta and back? Some people used to catch the bus to Asheville in the morning to go shopping and ride back in the afternoon. Times have changed.

Now this piece of nostalgia is not very important in the larger scheme of things. But if you reflect on what a group of young teenage girls thought was fun back then and compare it to the current generation, it does give you something to think about. Much has changed in the last sixty years; some might say we have lost those innocent years. I hope not.

HIGHLANDS' FIRST BASKETBALL TEAMS, 1948

It's basketball season in Highlands, and we thought you might like to know how it all got started at Highlands School. Back in 1948, Highlands may have fielded its first basketball teams. And if they weren't the first, they must have been some of the earliest. The old school sat up on the hill behind city hall, about where the ABC store is located now. Well, if you park behind city hall, where the public rest rooms are, that's where the first basketball court was located. It was hard-packed clay and sand, with a goal at each end and no roof. Imagine dribbling on that kind of surface. Baseball games were often called or rescheduled due to bad weather. Well, our home basketball games were also cancelled due to bad weather. No roof or walls.

That first year the coach was Reverend Robert DuPree. The school fielded both a boys' and a girls' team. Highlands played their first games against Hiawassee. There was a lot of excitement in both teams. Not just because it was our first game, but also because we were told that Hiawassee had a gym. There would be wood floors, walls and a roof. Back then there weren't any activity buses for the school's extra-curricular use—at least not the Highlands school. So both teams were going to ride in a big cabbage truck, with hay scattered in the truck bed, driven by one of the parents. It was cold going to that first game and even colder coming back. The smarter ones got to the front up against the truck cab to stay out of the wind. Since there were both boys and girls back there, I am sure that some romances may have begun or ended on those trips.

When we arrived at Hiawassee, we looked for the gym. All we saw beside the schoolhouse was a raised wooden platform with a roof supported by locust posts and no walls. A big disappointment. Reverend DuPree asked where the locker rooms were. The Hiawassee coach pointed to two paths leading into the woods away from the school. Reverend DuPree pointed the girls' team down one path and the boys' team down the other. At the end of each path was an outhouse. Those were the locker rooms. As the teams did not have uniforms yet, they changed into shorts and tops of various sizes and colors. It was quite a sight, and the Hiawassee team made great fun of us.

We thought that the wood floor would be an improvement over our court. Dribbling should be much better. But our first time on the floor proved different. Yes, it was wood, but it wasn't a smooth hardwood floor. The boards were uneven, and some were higher than others. The ball bounced high but also in whatever direction it wanted when it hit a crack or an uneven board. The dribbling of the ball on that raised floor made a very loud noise. Needless to say, the game was a disaster.

The next game was with Rosman, and by then both teams had uniforms. Since the shorts were very big in the legs, some of the girls took elastic and sewed it into the bottom hem of the shorts. Now those girls had bloomers. By this time, the parents and coaches had decided that a cabbage truck was

The 1948 girls' basketball team. *Back row, left to right*: Principal Otto Summer, Patsy Hayes, Elizabeth "Lifa" Newton, Mary Deas Anderson, Joyce Burnette, Isabel Hall and Reverend Robert B. "Bob" DuPree. *Front row, left to right*: Kathleen Potts, Martha Holt, Suzie Nix, Annie Nix, Evelyn Lewis and Anne Anderson.

The 1948 boys' basketball team. *Back row, left to right*: Charles Crunkleton, Dick "Duane" Edwards, Charlie Ray "Bo" Norton, Mack Hopper, Harry "Goog" Holt and Reverend Robert B. "Bob" DuPree. *Front row, left to right*: Neville Wilson, Arnold Keener, Bobby Houston, Paul Price and Bobby Potts.

not the best means of transportation. Those days were over. We used an old school bus that the Presbyterian church congregation had bought. From time to time that winter, we would ride in that bus. When we arrived in Rosman, we found a real enclosed gym with a hardwood floor. Everyone's game improved that night.

The next game was with Tamassee School near Salem, South Carolina, but we played it in the gym at Walhalla. I believe it was Louise Holt, Martha Holt's mother, who organized a car pool. Louise and her husband, Harry, had a taxi business in town, and she was used to driving a lot. A number of the other parents took turns, including Tudor and Margaret Hall and Charlie Anderson.

The pictures here show the teams. The girls' heights ranged from just under five feet to five feet, seven or eight inches. The boys started at around five, six and went to a little over six feet. You may notice that the boys look a little haggard, while the girls look fresh. That's because the pictures were taken after the boys' game and before the girls' game. As you will also notice, both teams made it to the Smoky Mountain Conference Gold Medal Tournament at Canton.

A CHRISTMAS EVE STORY AT INCARNATION

When we're asked if there'll be a white Christmas in Highlands, as we often are, the answer is usually, "Possibly, but we have a better chance of snow at Thanksgiving than Christmas." That's not to say we don't have white Christmases; it's just not a given. So we'd like to tell you about a family Christmas back in the early '60s.

This was when the Episcopal Church of the Incarnation was the only church in Highlands that had a Christmas Eve service. It was before the time when many of our summer residents returned for a family Christmas in Highlands. So a great number of members from other Highlands churches would attend. Isabel and I and our three sons were up from Atlanta for the holiday. We were staying at a large six-bedroom home on Satulah, as were her brother Bud and his family from Florida and her sister Sarah and her family from Greensboro. We filled the house along with their parents, Margaret and Tudor Hall, and grandmother, Gilbert. Brother John and his new wife were building their house in Highlands, and so they joined the rest of us. We had a full house: five families with seven children and grandmother Gilbert.

Christmas Day was on a Monday that year, which meant that Bud and his family had to drive back home to Florida on Christmas Day in order to be at work on Tuesday. A suggestion was made to celebrate Christmas a day early. Some parents thought that their children might figure the ruse out, but the majority ruled in favor of going ahead with the plan. We went out to get a tree on Saturday, and the adults decorated it after all of the children were in bed Saturday night, a Hall family tradition. The oldest child was only nine and hadn't a clue that we were a day early. Sunday morning was really hectic, with eighteen adults and children around the tree. The youngest was our son, Tim, who was not six months old. Under the tree were two sleds for our other two sons, Tucker and Tommy. Of course, they all thought there would be snow on the ground.

Memories of Days Gone By

The traditional turkey dinner followed, with Grandmother Gilbert doing a great job with granddaughters and granddaughters-in-law assisting. The group broke up after dinner, and some went to visit relatives and others looked after their children. Later on, Tudor asked who was going to church, and most of the other adults were skeptical. It was Father Gale Webbe's second Christmas in Highlands, and Tudor convinced everyone that the Hall clan should make a good showing. As the night approached, it began to rain, and several of us had second thoughts about staying up for a midnight service. When Grandmother Gilbert volunteered to look after the children, there wasn't much excuse not to go.

The temperature started to drop, but it really was a messy, rainy night as we drove down to church. When we walked into church, Father Webbe approached Isabel and took her off to the side. "Isabel, I understand that you played the organ for church back in the fifties. Our organist phoned me and can't make it. Do you suppose you could play tonight?"

By then, the church was filling up, and Isabel didn't know what to say. She had played the old pump organ when we lived here after college, but now there was a new electronic organ with foot pedals. She hesitated, and Father Webbe looked hopefully at her but didn't say a word. Finally she said, "All right, but please explain to the congregation about my—well, that I haven't played this organ before."

Needless to say, Isabel did very well. She didn't try to use the foot pedals, and the Christmas hymns were those that she'd played for years on the piano and the old pump organ. During the service, the wind began to howl and the rain stopped. Tudor went over to the furnace thermostat and set it higher, as the church was getting cold. Back then there wasn't any insulation in the walls or ceiling, and the old furnace was being put to the test to keep the outside air from taking over inside.

After communion, and just when we were going to sing the last hymn, the power went off and the lights went out. The altar candles became the only illumination in the church. The closing hymn was "Silent Night"—with an electronic organ that Isabel couldn't play. Except for the wind, it was very silent. Someone, we don't remember who, began the first line of the hymn, and then gradually everyone joined in. Miraculously, the starting pitch was good for all those singing, so we sang "Silent Night" a cappella. After Father Webbe gave the benediction, and as we filed out of church, it started to snow. A woman said as she stepped out the door, "My, it's all white outside!"

Margaret said in reply, "Yes and there's a lot of white inside, too," referring to all of the older generation. It snowed all night and into the morning. Bud and his family left early after checking with the Highway Patrol about the road conditions going south out of town. The rest of us went up Satulah Road with the two new sleds and one old sled that the children called "Red Devil." The children sledded all morning, and "Red Devil" was voted the best of the sleds. So much for new sleds. Finally, we had to pack up and head back to Atlanta and Greensboro.

THE GOOD OLD DAYS

I hope many of you remember the articles that Dr. Lee Copple wrote in the Highlander *some years back. Sometimes his ramblings went back in time, and others were more current. We enjoyed these stories. Perhaps there may have been a little too much use of his expression "My Good Wife," but then again it made an impression on us. We are taking you all back to a time in the life of Isabel and Tony, before we were married. It's really Isabel's story, so she'll be your narrator.*

Imagine most of the secondary roads back then, in the late 1940s, when they were either gravel or just plain dirt. Buck Creek Road was one of those that was graveled—barely. Tony's mother, Dayis Chambers Way, lived in a house that she and her second husband, Bill Way, had built just before World War II. Tony and his sister, Jan, were spending the summer with their mother, and Jan was dating Craig Cranston. So the scene is set for Craig to drive out with Colonel Ralph Mobray and his daughter, Ann, to dinner, while my father and mother, Tudor and Margaret Hall, drove me out. Two cars when one would do—a shameful waste of gas, but it was only about twenty-five cents per gallon then.

On the way out my father spotted a rattlesnake in the middle of the gravel road. Now my dad thought the snake would make a good specimen for the Highlands Biological Station museum, so he stopped the car. He took the lace out of one of his shoes, went to the side of the road, cut a branch with a forked end, cut another branch and tied the shoelace to the end of it with a loop slipknot. While mother and I watched, he walked over to the snake, keeping out of his striking range, caught the snake's head with the forked stick and then slipped the noose on the other stick over the its head. He asked me to open the trunk and get out a tow sack, a burlap bag, and bring it to him. As I held open the sack, he whirled the snake up and plopped him in the sack. After tying the top of the sack with his shoelace, he put snake, sack and shoelace in the trunk and we went on to the Way's. I'm glad I didn't have to go back with that snake in the trunk.

Day Way's dinner was delicious. There was food I had never had before. I think it was lamb curry with seven or eight side dishes over rice. Bill and Day were good hosts. After dinner, we played Monopoly. About ten o'clock, we said our goodbyes, as I was to ride back to town with Craig and the Mobrays. Right where the Buck Creek garbage and recycling center is now, there was a large rock almost in the middle of the road. It was necessary to drive on one side or the other unless you had a high clearance truck. Past that and before the bridge over Bad Branch there was a large truck with, I think, a broken axle. The road was narrow, and Craig thought he could drive around the truck, but there wasn't enough room and the road was muddy (remember it was barely gravel). He slid off the road and down the bank.

Two men tried to get the truck moving, but they weren't making any progress. Craig and the two men tried using a shovel to dig a path up to the road, but the car just slid farther down. Time went by, and then a pickup full of Webbs came around the curve heading home. They couldn't get by either, so all of the men including Craig literally picked up Craig's car and got it past the broken-down truck, while the Mobrays and I watched. By then my parents had called the Ways to find out if we were on our way home and were told that we'd been gone more than an hour. My father was starting out to find us when we arrived back home. I just had dinner with Tony, but the excitement coming and going was something I told him about the next day.

I hope this will give you some idea how life has changed in the past fifty years or more. Most people haven't seen a rattlesnake in the past twenty years or so, and almost all of the secondary roads are now paved—Turtle Pond, part of Dendy Orchard and Billy Cabin Road being some of the exceptions. How many men do you think it would take to pick up one our modern cars today?

"THE BOWERY, THE BOWERY"

Once again Isabel takes us down memory lane. Let her know if you have walked this path in the old days—before you get to the last paragraph.

One day in early June 1938, my grandmother asked my sister Sarah and I if we would like to go for a walk and picnic to the Bowery. We cried out, "Yes, sure! When do we go?"

We put on sturdy shoes while Grandmother (we called her Dama) prepared our picnic. We were soon ready. Dama carried a small picnic basket, while Sarah and I took turns carrying the thermos of Dama's wonderful punch. We left our house, turned right on Fifth Street, walked to Uncle Jack's home next door and took a path that led us through the pasture and straight to the tall white pines that surrounded the clay tennis court. The path went around the court and down a small incline in front of the Hall House Lake. There was a bridge downstream from the dam. As we crossed the bridge, we stopped and played "sticks," like Christopher Robin and Pooh. We would drop sticks on the upstream side of the bridge and run to the other side to see whose stick went under the bridge first.

Dama called to us, "We'd better get going or we will never get to the Bowery."

Off we went up a small hill to the Hall House that was at the top. It was a big two-story Dutch colonial house where my other grandmother Meta Norton Hall, lived. She and my grandfather Hall had run it as an inn, but by now it had been closed for some time. We didn't have time to stop, but she waved and told us to have fun when we told her we were going on a picnic.

The path led on past what everyone called "the shacks"—six small cabins that had been moved from Bug Hill. There were two cabins connected with a bath between them and had been used for inn guests. The path came to a barbwire fence (what city folks call "barbed wire") that headed toward Lindenwood Lake. Sarah and I crawled under it then held it up for Dama. Sixth Street was not open back then, and the path led to the lake. When we got to this part of the path, it got wider. There were tall white pines overhead, laurel and rhododendron all around us and millions of galax leaves at our feet. We went up a small hill and then stood on the shore of Lindenwood Lake. It was a beautiful spot with pink and white water lilies sitting on their large flat leaves and floating on top of the water.

We walked along the shore until we came to Lower Lake Road. It was wide and easy to walk on. After we passed the Rhododendron Trail, it got very rough with rocks everywhere. We didn't care, though, since we'd soon be to a small trail that went off to the left through a rhododendron and laurel thicket. Not far up that trail was a wishing well where we stopped to make a wish. Dama had pennies for us, and we made a wish. The wishing well was made of a round circle of stones, about a foot high and covered with moss. We called it a wishing well, but Dama said it must have been a spring reservoir at one time. We knew the water was good to drink because there was a black lizard in it. Sarah got a large rhododendron leaf and held both ends to make a cup. She dipped it into the water and I did the same. The water was cool and delicious.

Now we finished our short rest stop and started up the hill. We passed some pink lady slippers and trillium. Dama wouldn't let us pick them. She said they were happier being left to grow. Soon we came out on Bowery Road. There was one house on the right and one on the left. They were both were owned by families that had that same name but spelled differently: Evans and Evins. We just peeked through the bushes at the homes. Now the road had two wide ruts that were easy to walk on if you stayed in them.

We rounded a curve and came to two beautiful black wrought-iron gates hanging on big stone posts. It was Kalalanta. We knew it was haunted, so we ran past real fast. The next house we came to was old man Pierson's. The road stopped there and turned into a cow path, and we followed that. There were wildflowers all around us: Turk's-cap, Iris chrystada, Indian paintbrush and Pipsissawa. Soon we came to a swamp. As we got near, there were all kinds of splashing noise as frogs jumped off their logs into the water. We stopped and watched as they skewered into the water to hide from us, except one big shiny bullfrog that just sat and looked at us. Sarah pitched a small stone at him so he would jump in the water too. Here's where we saw Quaker Ladies, cattails and rushes. It was wet for walking, and our feet got wet, sturdy shoes or not.

Dama said, "Keep walking, we only have a little farther to go." Then she began to sing. She loved to sing since she had sung in the Mormon Tabernacle Choir in Salt Lake City, Utah, as a young woman. "The Bowery, the Bowery, they say such things and they do such things, I'll never go there anymore."

"Dama, why do you sing that?" Sarah asked.

"It's a song we used to sing when I got married. I thought you might like it. Now we're almost there. At our Bowery."

Sure enough, we turned off the cow path, though it kept going. Off to the right was a new path that was covered in pine needles with lots of rhododendron, laurel bushes and tall pines. Soon we came out of the woods to a big flat rock. There was a beautiful view of the mountains in the distance. I just knew if I could see better that I could see the ocean. We were standing on the Bowery. Dama made us sit down so we wouldn't run around and slip and fall over the cliff. We could see small houses and little lakes in the valley below.

Dama got the lunch that she had made out of the basket: banana sandwiches and my favorite, wild strawberry jam sandwiches. We put our cups in small holes in the rock to keep them from spilling. Then Dama poured our punch as we sat and looked at the view; we saw three falcons or hawks that were soaring on the currents from the valley below. Last, but best, she gave us each a fried apple pie. We sat there looking at the view and eating. We were stuffed. The sun was getting low, so Dama said that we had better start home. As we started back, Sarah started to sing Dama's song but changed the words: "The Bowery, the Bowery, we saw such things and we ate good things on the Bowery, the Bowery, we'll have to come back here some more."

Shall we take the same walk now, in present time? The field where we started has a house on it. The trees around the tennis court are gone and have been replaced with condominiums. The Hall House is gone along with the shacks that were moved to other locations. The Hall House Lake and dam are gone, swept away in the great storm of '39. More condominiums were built there, too. There is a new street, Sixth Street, which has changed the landscape of Lindenwood Lake. The road is wider with lots of traffic. It's hard to find the trail to the wishing well, now just a pile of rocks with a little pool of water. Bowery Road is in the process of being widened and paved. Many of the houses along the way, like Kalalanta and old man Pierson's, are almost the same. The wildflowers are gone, the swamp has a culvert and there are no frogs jumping into the water.

THE DAY FDR CAME TO HIGHLANDS—SORT OF

Momma was running back and forth between our bedroom and my brother's, fussing over our clothes. "Hurry children, we don't want to miss President Roosevelt." Yes, the day had finally arrived. We were all going to see the president of the United States. Our teachers at Highlands School had been preparing us for this event.

You see, President Franklin Delano Roosevelt was going to dedicate the Great Smoky Mountain National Park and come through Highlands on his way back from the dedication. It was September 2, 1940. We were going out to Big View, the overlook near Whiteside Mountain. Dama, our grandmother, had been busy since breakfast making sandwiches and punch to take with us. She put the sandwiches in a dress box and the punch in a brown and yellow gallon thermos with a spigot. My sister Sarah and I were dressed alike in white dresses with pink sashes and black Mary Jane shoes with white socks. My brother Buddy had white shorts and a blue shirt. Momma made it very clear that we were not to get our clothes dirty and to behave like little ladies and gentlemen.

We rode out to Big View in our Dodge: Dama, Daddy, Momma, Sarah, Buddy and I. Momma wanted to be out there first and get the best parking spot because it would be very crowded. But there were several cars that beat us, and Momma had a hard time deciding where Daddy should park. Sarah, Buddy and I got out while Dama and Daddy set up our picnic. Momma fussed around, mostly trying to decide the best place to be when the president came by.

We got hungry and persuaded Momma to let us go ahead and eat. We weren't really that hungry, but since we couldn't play, it was something to do. Every time a car came up the road from Cashiers, someone would shout, "Here he comes." The car would drive by, people would wave and the people in the car would wave back, but it wasn't the president.

By now, it seemed like everyone in town was here, and it was getting hot. Sarah and I were getting restless, and Buddy had already started playing on the bank above the road. Momma was watching down the highway and wasn't paying any attention to us. So we joined Buddy and got down on our knees. Buddy had brought some of his metal cars, and we started building roads. We must have played for several hours, and by then our sashes had fallen off, our Mary Jane's were all scuffed and Momma was really upset. Not about us; the president hadn't come. People started back to town. After a while, Momma told Daddy to pack up the picnic things. We were going home. They never did tell us why the president didn't come.

WINTER: TIME FOR ICE CREAM

It was a cold Saturday morning, and we were all eating breakfast. Daddy looked around the table and asked, "Who would like some ice cream?"

Naturally Sarah, Buddy and I shouted, "We do."

A strange reaction for us to have, you might say. Earlier I had looked at the outdoor thermometer and it showed fifteen degrees. Not your typical hot summer day when ice cream would taste great. But this was Highlands, and

Ice tags on the rock overhangs on Cashiers Road.

whenever it got cold and icy, there would be large icicles hanging down from the rock outcroppings on the roadsides.

Just then Sarge Gibson came in the back porch door carrying a large pail of fresh milk from our cow. We called him "old Sarge," although he was about thirty. He was my dad's helper in his plumbing and electric business, but he also milked and fed our cow every morning and evening.

"Mrs. Gilbert, the milk seems awful thick today. Maybe more cream than usual."

"Thank you Sarge. Just sit it there on the back porch. I believe Tudor has just thought of a good use for it today."

We finished up breakfast awfully fast after that. Daddy told us to get dressed warmly, and he went out to start the truck. Sarah and I went upstairs, while Buddy finished the bacon and scrambled eggs that were left. While Buddy went to get warmer clothes on, Sarah and I went out to Daddy's shop to get the single-bit axe and several empty feed sacks that were kept on the left side of the door going into the shop.

We all got into the front seat of the truck, and Daddy drove out Cashiers Road. When we got underneath Little Bear Pen, he pulled off to the side of the road, and we all got out. There were big, long icicles hanging from the rocks. Sarge called them ice tags, and we thought that was kind of neat. We tried to pull off some, and from those we couldn't Daddy knocked off chunks with the axe. We would pick them up and put them in the sacks, but we couldn't pick up the sacks when they were full. They had old leaves and sometimes moss on them, but we knew that wouldn't make any difference. We had so much fun doing it that we were kind of disappointed when Daddy said we had enough. But if the truth be told, we were all freezing and ready to get home.

Mother and Grandmother were ready for us when we got back. They had gotten out the ice cream churn and filled it with thick, fresh, warm cream. Daddy took the sacks out on the back porch and beat the icicles into small pieces. Then he poured the cracked ice into the sides of the churn and added rock salt after each layer of ice. When he decided it was ready to crank the churn, Sarah, Bud and I all wanted to crank. We all took turns cranking. It was easy at first, but when it got harder Daddy would take over. Our real job was to sit on the churn to keep the can of cream from floating. When it was finished, he unhooked the crank apparatus from the can. Then he looked around and asked, "Who wants to lick the dasher?"

Of course we all did, so it was up to Grandmother to play a game to select the first and second lickers. After that, we all sat down to a small table just for us, and Grandmother brought us each a dish of ice cream and a mug of hot chocolate. We had an electric refrigerator but no freezer—just a small two-tray space for ice cubes. So making ice cream in the winter was the only time we could have it.

That's what we call winter: time for ice cream.

END OF THE RAINBOW

This is a story that I think some young children growing up in Highlands in the 1930s and '40s can relate to: a meeting between summer residents and their children and local children.

Times have changed since then, but many of those friendships have continued to this day. The house described here was called World's End. It was the last house up Satulah Mountain and was built by Robert B. Eskrigge, a native of Cheshire, England, and resident of New Orleans, Louisiana, near the beginning of the last century.

It was a beautiful summer day in July. My sister Sarah and I had been invited out to dinner (called lunch now). We were going to meet a new friend and go to her grandparents' house on Satulah. She was our age, and our mother and her mother thought it would be a good thing, but I was nervous. I was very shy, and going to a house I'd never been to and meeting new people terrified me. So I tried to pretend that I was sick and couldn't go.

I was sitting on my bed when mother came in the room. "Isabel, you have got to get dressed. Sarah is downstairs ready to go. Come on now, don't be afraid. I'm sure you will like Mary and her mother and grandparents. Now, let me see what would be good for you to wear?" So that was that; I was going. She selected a pale blue dress with small pink and green flowers. It had a flat, round collar, puffed sleeves and a gathered skirt with a big sash in the back. Then she picked a dark blue cardigan sweater to go with it. Back then it was cool in July, and you never left home without a sweater. Finally, she handed me a pair of two-buckle, white leather sandals with leather soles and white socks to keep my feet warm.

After much combing of my hair and getting my white hair bow just right, I passed my mother's inspection. I was ready. When I went downstairs, Sarah was sitting at the dining room table, looking real cute in her Dutch boy–cut blonde hair. She had already finished breakfast, but Dama had saved me some eggs and bacon. I almost gagged but got some of it down. I was in terror of going up on the mountain for dinner, with everyone a stranger except Sarah. I didn't know why mother or Dama weren't going. On the other hand, Sarah was excited. She looked on it as another adventure. Mother came in and said we had fifteen minutes to be ready.

So I went upstairs to brush my teeth and get my sweater. I took the full fifteen minutes looking at movie star pictures that we wrote off for. Then mother called from downstairs that they were here. I looked out our bedroom window and saw a big shiny green Chevrolet touring car pull up in front of our house. Oh my, I guess this is it!

"Come on!" Sarah shouted and ran out the door.

Mother took my hand, and we walked down to the street. Sarah was already standing there in her pink dress. A tall young girl got out of the back seat and stood next to an older woman, about Dama's age. Another younger woman got out of the driver's seat and came around the car.

"Margaret, I'd like you to meet my mother, Virginia, and my daughter, Mary." Edith said.

The Eskrigge home on Satulah Mountain.

Interior of the Eskrigge home.

"I'm pleased to meet you Virginia. These are my daughters, Sarah and Isabel," Mother replied, and Sarah curtsied. Always the showoff.

"Well, you girls have a good time," Mother said as Sarah jumped in the back seat with Mary. I had to crawl over Sarah to get in the middle. Mary and Sarah giggled, and I realized right then that I was the odd one. Mary's mother got in the driver's seat and turned around to see us. "Well girls, we're off for a fine day."

She was so nice. I knew everything would be OK. She drove through the center of town between Edwards Hotel and Highlands Inn with no stoplights to slow us down. Then she turned up the hill; up and up we went. The road got rougher and bump, bump, bump we went. Sometimes the car almost stalled until Mary's mother shifted gears. We went around two hairpin turns. I couldn't see where we were going. Mary and Sarah had their heads out the windows, and I couldn't see out the front. All I could tell is that it was a rough road. Finally we stopped, and both Sarah and Mary jumped out of each side of the car and waited for Mary's mother and grandmother to get out.

When I got out, there was a stone wall in front of the car, as well as the largest gray stone house I had ever seen. It looked like a castle. It had a steep pointed roof, and I was only looking at the end. What must the front look like, I wondered? It was scary, too. There were tall hemlock hedges leading to a door.

On Mary's side of the car there was chicken house. She told us to come and feed the chickens, so off we went into the fenced yard with chickens everywhere. At one end of the chicken house there were all kinds of tools: rakes, hoes, watering cans and a wheelbarrow. Mary took the top off a large lard can and told us to get a handful of corn. I got one handful and Sarah got two, and we went back into the yard. We threw the corn on the ground, and the chickens went wild, but after a bit they calmed down. Sarah wanted to get some more, but Mary told her we couldn't because the chickens would blow up. Of course we had chickens at our house, and I knew that wasn't true. Mary's grandfather probably told her that to keep her from feeding the chickens too much.

"Come on, follow me, Sarah," Mary said, and off they went as I ran to catch up.

I followed them back to where the car was parked and around to the gray stone wall. There were three large stones that stuck out from the wall. Mary said they were steps, and she went up them with Sarah following and then me. When we got to the top of the wall, the ground was level, and there was a clay tennis court with a bench on one side with two tennis rackets and a couple of balls. Mary and Sarah each took a racket, and Mary said I could be the ball boy. This gave me the chance to explore around the court. On the far side of the court, the mountain rose up with big, beautiful moss-covered rocks. In the middle of the rocks there was a cold, dark spring flowing into a sort of hollow crevasse with a watermelon floating in it. I picked up a tin dipper lying next to it and took a drink. When I did, Sarah and Mary saw me, ran over and wanted the dipper. I was through with it anyway, so I gave it to Mary. She took a drink and gave it to Sarah. All the time they were arguing about how to play and keep score. Sarah said she knew because she played tennis on the court that was in our backyard. It was left from the Hall House Hotel. She learned how to keep score from the grownups that would come to play. Mary said that she had not played that much, so maybe we'd better do something else.

Mary led us back toward the house across a big, flat lawn. There was a tall stone wall on the upper side and another on the lower side, but I tripped on some wire hoop and fell on the ground. "Come on, Isa," Sarah called out. "Mary wants us to meet her grandfather."

I got up and brushed myself off and followed them to the front of the house. There was an older man standing there, propped by a stick. He was dressed in tweed knickers with high wool socks and a tweed jacket with leather patches on the sleeves. His hair was white and he had a gray beard. He looked down at us and said, "Hello there young ladies. How are you? Mary, introduce me to your friends."

"Grandfather, this is Isabel and Sarah. Mother and Grandmother have invited them to dinner," Mary explained.

"Well," he said, "I'm happy to have you here. It won't be long until dinner, so stay close so you can hear the bell. I think I'll go back inside, it's getting a little chilly out here." He reached around behind him and took the stick. It had a sort of seat that he folded up, and then he used it as a cane.

Mary said she wanted to show us the quarry, so we walked across the lawn in front of the house. The house was two stories tall with granite dormers. There was a stone terrace with an arbor over it just full of vines, roses, ivy and clematis to provide shade. Under the arbor there were several red rocking chairs. I wanted to sit down, but Mary wanted us to see the rock quarry, whatever that was. We walked down to the edge of the grass terrace and then along the wall, trying not to fall off on the one side or step on the flowers on the upper side. When the wall ended, we took a trail into the woods, through laurel and rhododendron and over galax-covered ground.

Then the woods opened up; there was a clearing with high, gray rock cliffs. At the foot of the cliffs were more rocks: some square and some with flat sides. Mary said that this was where they got the rocks to build the house. They quarried it; that's why it was called a quarry. I learned a new word and its meaning that day.

We sat down and talked about the butterflies and the birds for a while, and then Mary asked if we would like to see the barn. Sarah asked if they had horses. She loved horses. Mary said they didn't have horses anymore. There used to be some when the house was first built. So we walked back down the trail to the terrace and stumbled over these wire things stuck in the grass. Mary said that they were for playing croquet. "What's that?" I asked.

Mary said, "I'll tell you later." And off she went down some of those rock steps in the terrace wall, just like at the tennis court. Now we were in a wildflower field with a trail leading to an old road. Mary went first, Sarah second and then me. Snakes always bite the third one, I had heard. Oh my, and me with nothing but my white leather sandals for protection. But soon we got to the old road where I could see my feet, and I felt better. At the end of the road was a big old barn. It was two stories high, with old gray wood that looked like it had never been painted. When we went inside it was dark and smelled of old hay, and you could almost smell horses and leather. When my eyes got used to the little light from the door, I could see that there were saddles, bridles, stirrups and pitchforks. Best of all there was an old carriage with leather seats, a whip in its socket and two kerosene lamps near the front.

Mary jumped up on the carriage seat and said, "Come on, let's go somewhere." So Sarah and I got up on the wide seat and bounced as the Indians chased us down the mountain like in the Tom Mix movies we saw at the school auditorium. When we bounced, the dust on the seats flew up. We were having so much fun, and then we heard the sound of a bell in the distance. Mary jumped down and said, "Dinner." We followed her out of the barn, up the old road to the trail. I made sure I was second, behind Mary. Let the snakes get Sarah.

When we got to the wall, we ran up the funny stone steps and across the terrace to where Mary's grandfather was sitting in one of the rockers. He got up and said with a smile, "Good. You are on time and Cook is waiting."

We followed him inside to a hallway with stairs at the far end and a huge grandfather clock bonging twelve times. I looked up at the tall ceiling. The walls were plaster like our upstairs walls, but the wood trim was quite large. We walked down the wood-floored hall to a large living room with a fireplace and fire going. Mary's mother and grandmother were seated on opposite sides of the fireplace, and her grandfather pointed to several chairs for us to sit in. The room was huge. It seemed as big as our church, but I know it couldn't have been that large. We had no sooner sat down than a tall, robust woman came in. She wore a white apron and a white cap, sort of like a nurse.

"Dinner is served," she said to everyone.

"Well, Cook, that's right on time. Come on young ladies, you too, Edith and Virginia. We mustn't keep Cook waiting."

We went into a large dining room, much larger than ours, and sat at a big table. It could have seated lots of people. The table was set with silver and china and had a flower arrangement of dahlias in the middle. Mary's grandmother went to one end of the table, and her grandfather went to the other after seating her. Mary and Sarah went to the far side of the table and Mary's mother led me to the near side. There were tremendous, flat soup bowls already at each place. I barely could see over the top of the table, and I watched Mary so I would pick the right spoon. She picked the one on the outside, and I gasped. It was as big as the spoons Dama used to serve vegetables at home. I straightened up as tall as I could in the chair and picked up the large spoon. It was really hard to get any soup into it, but I tried as best I could. After the soup, Mary's grandmother rang a tiny bell, and Cook came in with a smile on her face and laughter in her voice. She took our bowls and brought us our dinner. It was chicken-a-la king with small green peas and a very good fruit salad. Then we had cold watermelon for dessert. All during dinner everyone talked and laughed, so it all went well. Sarah and I both made sure we told Mary's mother and grandparents how good the dinner was. When we finished, Mary asked if we could be excused, and then we went into the living room.

It had started raining during dinner, so it left us with no place to play except inside. Mary suggested that we play hide-and-seek.

Then she said, "I know, we'll draw to see who's it." We started the chant "one potato, two potato, three potato, four." Guess who lost? I was it. I sat in the living room, put my head down, closed my eyes and started counting. I heard the scampering of feet as Mary and Sarah ran to hide. Five, ten, fifteen, twenty I counted to myself. Then at one hundred, I got up and shouted, "Here I come, ready or not!" I ran down the hall toward the stairs. I thought I had heard them clattering up the stairs. At least I thought that was what I heard. The stairs didn't have a runner like the hall, so that must have been them. I tried to tiptoe up, but my sandals still made a clatter. When I got to the top, there was long hall going back each way. Across the hall I saw the rain outside through the dormer windows. It was really coming down in buckets. I shivered. I wanted this to be over. It was a scary old house. Which way did they go? Then I saw a door down at the left end of the hall that was open a crack. I tiptoed down, staying on the hall runner. When I got to the door, I pushed it open slowly. The room was big with windows on three sides. There was a fire in the fireplace. Gosh, they have a fire in the middle of summer. But it was a cold sort of house anyway. I peeked around the door and didn't see anyone, so I slowly pulled the door almost closed and turned back toward the hall. There were doors on the stair side and tall windows on the other side that were set back almost a foot or more. It was then that I realized how thick the outside walls must be.

I tiptoed back down the hall and tried one door that was open a crack. When I opened it, I saw a large tub on legs, a sink on a pedestal and a toilet with a tank up high on the wall with a chain hanging down. Then there was a loud "Boo!" as one of them jumped from behind the door. Just then there was a clap of thunder and lightning that filled the room with light and noise. I pulled my sweater over my head just as a white ghost passed in front of me. I was just pulling my sweater back when it thundered again, and a big white thing passed in front of my face. I pulled my sweater over my head and face again, and then I heard giggling and two bodies pushed past me and ran down the hall. When I got my sweater back straight, I saw my big white hair bow on the floor. That was what I saw, and I thought it was a ghost. Oh, I wanted to get out of that big house. I slowly retreated down the hall and steps. Mary, Sarah and Mary's mother and grandmother were standing at the bottom as I turned on the landing.

"I think it's time to take you and Sarah back to the village. You seemed to have a full time of it," Mary's mother said. She was smiling with almost a grin. I didn't know then what that was all about. Of course, Mary and Sarah were giggling, but they seemed to be doing that all the time. Being the little sister brought its own problems.

When we walked out the front door, I looked out at the far mountains. There was a mist between them and the valley below. Then I saw a beautiful rainbow that stretched from the valley and came down right at the house. It was beautiful, and where it came down the grass was sparkling like diamonds where the sudden shower had left droplets of rain.

We all got into the car. Mary's grandfather waved from the patio and then walked back into the house. I sat in the middle again, but as we drove off I stood up and looked out the rear window. The rainbow was still there, coming right down on the stone walls of the castle. Everyone was quiet except Mary and Sarah. They kept turning toward me and giggling. When we got home, we thanked Mary and her mother for a nice day and dinner. Sarah looked the same as she did when we left. Then mother came up the walk, and the first thing she said was, "Isabel, what happened to you?" My hair was a mess from all those dives under my sweater. So now it was stretched four sizes bigger. It hung all over me.

I told her that nothing happened. It had been a good day. I couldn't tell what really happened. She wouldn't understand.

THE GREAT STORM OF 1939

The following information comes, in part, from the National Oceanic and Atmospheric Administration's (NOAA) historical hurricane records found on the Internet.

It was on Labor Day in September 1939 when storm number two came out of the east Caribbean from the Atlantic Ocean. It ran in a northwesterly direction above Puerto Rico, staying well clear of the Island of Santo Domingo and Cuba. Then it struck the east coast of Florida in the Fort Pierce–Palm Beach area and continued in the same northwesterly direction, cutting diagonally across the state and entering the Gulf of Mexico north of Tampa. The next landfall was about at Cape St. George on the coast of the Florida panhandle. Maximum winds for the storm were eighty miles per hour. Entering southern Alabama with still strong winds and rain, it almost got to the Louisiana line before it turned northeast and headed for Highlands, North Carolina.

Back then, there were no hourly updates from a hurricane weather center and no TV weather people reporting on the hurricane. The storm was tracked from behind the curve. Radio stations broadcast what had happened, not what was going to happen. When it got to the mountains, the rainfall and winds must have been high.

There are many people in Highlands who remember the storm. Here are two accounts from your authors. First, Tony: My sister Jan and I were in our parents' home on Buck Creek Road. Sarah Crunkleton was with us.

Washed-out highway after the 1939 hurricane.

The power went first. We had no phone, so we didn't lose that service. Our parents, Overton and Dayis Chambers, were in Chicago and had no idea of how we were or what the storm had done to us. Mother decided that she would drive to Highlands. The normal driving time was two days on two-lane roads for 725 miles. She didn't run into any problems until she was in North Carolina. At one point near Rosman, she was stopped by the Highway Patrol due to a washout. She convinced the officer that she could drive on a nearby railroad trestle and did so. She made it to Cashiers and then came up the Highlands Road, which also had several washouts that took away the outside lane. Coming up Buck Creek Road, the bridge at Bad Branch was out, and she walked the rest of the way. It took her twelve hours to make the trip, driving straight through.

Isabel was living in her home on Fifth Street, which crosses Mill Creek. Mill Creek's headwaters are above Lindenwood Lake. When that dam went out, it started a chain reaction. Now there are two more bridges over Mill Creek, one on Fifth Street and the other at US 64, and they washed out, too. All of this water and debris then headed for Mirror Lake and the Mirror Lake Bridge—the biggest of all though it could not withstand the torrent.

Billy, my family's pony, became frightened during the storm with all the thunder and lightning and ran away. After the storm, he was found on the far side of Mill Creek on Fifth Street and would not come back. A young man by the name of Fredrick ("Freddy") Sebastian Kurtina, who lived at

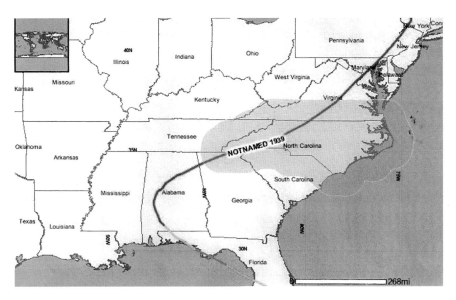

National Oceanic and Atmospheric Administration (NOAA) map of the 1940 hurricane.

the far end of the street near where Richard Melvin's mother lived, took Billy by his halter and walked him through the turbulent waters of the creek back home.

Highlands witnessed the winter "Storm of the Century" in March 1993 and the drubbing of Hurricane Opal in October 1995, but I believe that there was more damage done by storm number two in August 1939 than by either of the other two storms.

Bad Branch is located between the Big Creek Bridge and Simon Speed Road. The bridge has been replaced by a culvert. Lindenwood Lake is now called Ravenel Lake and is part of the Highlands Biological Station. There are at least two more Ravenel Lakes in the Highlands area.

PART II

INTERESTING PEOPLE

We are fortunate to have so many fascinating personages who either visited or were residents of our town. As you read over the stories about some of these individuals, you may come to a conclusion once voiced by Reverend Charles Bryan some years ago, who felt that there was some power, perhaps a magnetic force that drew so many people of varied backgrounds to Highlands.

THE NORTONS

For well over 126 years, descendants of Barak and Mary Nicholson Norton have gathered on a Sunday in July at the old white schoolhouse in Whiteside Cove. The Norton family is one of our oldest families in Highlands, Cashiers and the Norton community. The ancestor of all these Nortons was Edward Norton I. He was a native of County Armagh, Ireland. Two of his children, Edward II and Mary, moved from Ireland to America probably in the early 1700s. They landed in Pennsylvania in an area that later became part of Maryland. They were or became Quakers, as Quaker meetinghouse records indicate in their marriages records.

Edward Norton II and his family then moved to Virginia and later to North Carolina. A son, William, was born in North Carolina, married and reared a family. The family later moved to the Pickens District in South Carolina.

David and Mattie Norton.

Interesting People

One of William I's children was Barak Norton, who was born in 1777 in North Carolina but moved with his parents to South Carolina. Barak is the progenitor of all the Nortons in this area. His tale tells us a lot about early life in Western North Carolina.

He married Mary Nicholson from Tamassee Creek, South Carolina, near where the Nortons lived. They had nine children before Barak headed for the hills of North Carolina. As the story goes, he could see Whiteside Mountain from his home in Tamassee and decided to find it. At that time, there were Cherokee Indians living in Whiteside Cove. They had been pushed north out of South Carolina by the growing white settlements there.

The Cherokee befriended Barak and helped him set up his homestead. He returned to Tamassee and brought some slaves and his sons to carve out a farm. He then brought his large family into the Cove. In 1828, a daughter, Sarah, was born. She was the first white child born in the area and was given Whiteside as her middle name after the mountain that loomed above their homestead.

Barak and Mary had two more children in the cove, making a total of twelve in all. Some ten years later, the army came with orders to move the Cherokee west to Oklahoma, the infamous "Trail of Tears." An officer by the name of John Alley was in charge of the troop and asked Barak to help them round up the Cherokee. Because Barak knew all the cliffs and caves where they could be hiding, he helped the army. We don't know how Barak felt about this task at the time, but is it said that in later years he felt that he had done wrong to his Cherokee friends.

Colonel John Alley apparently liked Whiteside Cove and the surrounding country. When he retired from the army, he returned to Whiteside Cove, married Sarah Whiteside Norton and settled there. They had thirteen children. One of the most notable was their youngest, Judge Felix Eugene Alley.

There are hundreds of descendants of Barak and Mary. They have settled in Highlands, Cashiers and the Norton community, as well as all over the country. David Norton, a grandson of Barak and a Civil War veteran, was one of the early settlers in Highlands and owned the Central House. He was also a founding member of the Episcopal church in Highlands. So come July in the cove, many descendants of the Nortons gather for a family reunion to exchange genealogical information, now on CDs or floppies, as well as have an old-fashioned picnic on the ground.

For more information on the family, we suggest the following reading: *My Life and Times* by Thomas "Tom" Picklesimer, *Western North Carolina: A History from 1730 to 1913* by John Preston Arthur and *Random Thoughts and Musings of a Mountaineer* by Judge Felix Eugene Alley.

Some of Highlands' More Notable Visitors

Many times, we have heard or read this expression: "Highlands is the best-kept secret." This may be true, but if you keep repeating this, it no longer is much of a secret. Our founding fathers, C.C. Hutchinson and Samuel T. Kelsey, didn't want to keep it a secret, and for over one hundred years, the area has attracted a wide variety of very interesting personages.

One of the earliest people couldn't be classified a visitor, but he should be one of the notables regardless. This young man walked from Pennsylvania one summer and ended up in Highlands. Oh yes, and he walked back that same summer. When he got home, he found a letter waiting for him, asking if he would come back and head the local school. He was seventeen or eighteen at the time. He did return, and he not only ran the school, he also started a newspaper. He went on to finish his education in Europe as a botanist, assisted in the gardens of the Biltmore Estate and became a professor at North Carolina State University. His name is Professor Thomas G. Harbison.

Around the turn of the last century, 1898 to be exact, a botany professor from Clemson University brought a recent émigré from Glasgow, Scotland, to Highlands for their wedding. Back then, it was a two-day trip by horse and buggy. Ten years later, the couple built a home in Highlands. Besides the house, there was a windmill to raise water from his well, a barn, an icehouse, a two-story servants' house and a tennis court. They landscaped the grounds with all species of southern trees and shrubs and heather from Scotland. The house contained many of his inventions, such as glass bottles with colored liquid that served as fire extinguishers. The family later moved to Minnesota, where the professor had grown up. During this period, he invented and patented puffed wheat and puffed rice. His grandchildren and their children still have homes in Highlands. His name was Dr. Alexander P. Anderson, and his wife, from Glasgow, Scotland, was Lydia McDougal Johnson.

Then there was Dr. Mary Lapham, a world authority on the treatment of tuberculosis. She came to Highlands about 1902 and later opened a tuberculosis sanatorium, which attracted a **number of patients** from all over the country. Her treatment, called the Swiss method, was to collapse one lung. It must have worked because many of her patients, who came to Highlands for treatment but expected to die, survived and became some of our pioneers. Many outlived those who were not suffering from the disease. The sanatorium was called "Bug Hill" by the locals. It is now the site of the Highlands Civic Center.

Back in the 1930s and '40s, there was a very distinguished-looking gentleman who spent the summers in Highlands. His name was Newton McCully. He was of average build, had a white mustache and beard and usually was dressed in tweeds, sometimes with plus fours or knickers. He had had an interesting career in the U.S. Navy and served as naval military attaché in Russia during and after the Revolution.

From a book entitled *Stamping Out the Virus: The Allied Intervention in the Russian Civil War 1918–1920*, we found the following report:

> *The USS* Whipple *(DD217) arrived at Sevastopol on the morning of 14 November 1920 and reported to Vice Admiral Newton McCully for orders. Hundreds of boats scurried about the harbor, often crammed to the gunwales with fleeing White Russians. In addition to* Whipple, *cruiser* St. Louis *and two destroyers—*Overton *(DD-239) and* Humphreys *(DD-236)—stood by to evacuate selected individuals bearing passes from Admiral McCully. During the entire time* Whipple *remained at the doomed port, her main battery was trained out and manned. Armed boat crews carried evacuees out to the ship while her landing force stood in readiness. As her last boatload pushed off from shore, Bolshevik troops reached the main square and began firing on the fleeing White Russians;* Whipple *had been just ahead of the Reds.* Whipple *then towed a barge loaded with wounded White Russian troops out of range of the Bolshevik guns and then turned the tow over to the* Humphreys. *As* Whipple *passed* Overton, *Vice Admiral McCully, on the latter's bridge, called out by megaphone: "Well done,* Whipple.*" The last American vessel out of Sevastopol, the destroyer headed for Constantinople with her passengers, both topside and below decks. Each carried pitifully few belongings, had no food and very little money. Many were sick and wounded.*

There were many orphaned children during that time, and Admiral McCully did his best to help many of them. He personally adopted seven boys and girls and brought them back to the United States. Although a bachelor, he raised all of them, sent them to college and gave them a life they would not have had. One of his favorite pastimes was dancing at Helen's Barn. He didn't square dance, but in between sets he would take a partner and dance to a waltz on the jukebox.

During that same period, a well-known amateur golfer and Atlanta attorney had a summer home at Highlands Country Club. He attended local gatherings and was a true gentleman. Today, the only golf match allowed to use his name is the Highlands-Cashiers Hospital fundraiser with current and former Walker Cup players and other amateurs. His name, as you may have guessed, was Robert "Bobby" Jones.

In a twist of fate, we learned recently that an employee at the Fireside Restaurant had been the recipient of the Carnegie Medal for bravery. He had rescued a motorist trapped in a burning car. The twist of fate, you ask? Fireside Restaurant is on the property called Wright Square, and many know the story of Charlie Wright. He was a recipient of the Carnegie Medal almost one hundred years ago for saving the life of Gus Baty, who fell off the cliff at Whiteside Mountain. There are many more stories of visitors and our pioneer families. We hope you are able to attend "Walk in the Park" in the summer of each year, where amateur actors portray the lives of some of our notable pioneers. The event is sponsored and written by our own Highlands Historical Society.

HARLAN P. KELSEY

There have been a number of botanists, horticulturists and lovers of our trees, plants and shrubs over the years. Some came long before Highlands was established, and a number arrived afterward. This mecca of botanical search and research probably culminated in the founding of the Highlands Biological Station. Early visitors to our area were William Bartram and André Michaux in the late eighteenth and early nineteenth centuries. Later, after Highlands became a town, there were others, both professional and amateur botanists, including Professor Thomas G. Harbison, Henry Wright, Professor Lindsay Olive, Dr. Ralph Sargent and many, many more.

As it happens, though, one of the co-founders of Highlands, Samuel Truman Kelsey, was also interested in our varied and unusual flora. His son, Harlan, was only three years old when the family moved to Highlands from Kansas. They lived with Stanhope Hill in Horse Cove while Sam Kelsey

Highlands' first string quartet. *Left to right*: Frank Sheldon, Louis Zoellner, S.T. Kelsey Jr. and Harlan P. Kelsey.

built their home on the south side of Main Street across from the present Hudson Library. His property stretched back behind the house where he built a lake, which at various times was known as Kelsey Lake, Harbison Lake and now Harris Lake, all names that are a part of Highlands' rich heritage. The lake was primarily used for the large nursery he started, which specialized in our native trees and shrubs.

Harlan apparently showed enough interest in the nursery to prompt his father to set aside a quarter acre or so for his own nursery. As a result, Harlan prepared a mail order catalogue and became the youngest nurseryman in the country. When the Kelseys moved to an area north and east of Asheville near Grandfather Mountain and founded the town of Linville, the nursery was left in the hands of Thomas F. Parker, the son of Mrs. Prioleau Ravenel by her first marriage. Again, father and son, now a grown man of twenty, set up a nursery in 1892 in Linville, which was called Highlands Nursery after their first in our town.

Sometime before 1900, Harlan moved to Salem, Massachusetts. He first advertised in a Boston publication from 1898 until 1903 under his own name as a "Landscape Architect," using Highlands Nursery and Western North Carolina and Hardy American Ornamentals in the copy. In 1902, he married Florence Low. Soon after that, he went into partnership with another nurseryman, but when that partnership broke up, in 1910, Harlan renamed his nursery the Kelsey-Highlands Nursery with its location in East Boxford, Massachusetts. He continued to operate his nursery in Linville until 1920.

Along with his business enterprises, which took him all over the eastern United States and particularly back to the Carolinas, he became interested in conservation. He was a founder of the Appalachian Mountain Club. Linda Laderoute writes in her biography of Harlan Kelsey that "[i]n 1924, he was appointed to a Congressional Study Committee…to research appropriate land for a National Park in the eastern United States." There is no doubt that Kelsey's knowledge and love of the southeastern mountains was instrumental in directing the activities of the committee.

"The Great Smoky Mountains in North Carolina, Mammoth Caves in Kentucky and the Blue Ridge of Virginia were selected." Laderoute continues:

> By an act of Congress in 1925, a commission was appointed to define the boundaries of the proposed eastern parks. The same committee set forth to complete this task. Their delineation received Congressional approval in an act signed on March 22, 1926. Kelsey was also instrumental in the acquisition of the land, which was done by the states involved. This was completed in 1930 and then the committee was dissolved. The Great Smoky Mountain National Park and the Shenandoah National Park were added to the list of "national treasures" forever protected as worthy natural and scenic resources.

President Franklin Delano Roosevelt dedicated the Great Smoky Mountain National Park on September 2, 1940. He was supposed to come through Highlands after the dedication but never made it.

It was only by chance that we found out more about this son of Highlands. A gentleman by the name of Loren M. Wood came by our office one day after being referred by the chamber of commerce. He had purchased the property of Kelsey's Boxford, Massachusetts nursery and became interested in Kelsey. He followed his roots down to Highlands and gave us a copy of the Linda Laderoute biography of Harlan P. Kelsey. More recently, Judith Kelsey Long, granddaughter of S.T. Kelsey, daughter of S.T. Kelsey Jr. and grand-niece of Harlan P. Kelsey visited Highlands for the first time. This author took her to see the Kelsey monument at the corner of Fifth and Church Streets and also by Sue Potts to see plantings at her house in Sunset Hills, which was a part of the original Kelsey nursery.

ELBERT AND BESSIE: A TRANSCONTINENTAL STORY

This is the story of two of our earlier residents. Their backgrounds were totally different by religion, profession and geography. Yet they met, fell in love and became an important part of the fabric of early Highlands. People today think nothing of flying to various parts of our country, traveling to visit relatives and friends, to attend business meetings or just for fun. One hundred years back, trains provided our means of travel, both coast to coast or to the next state. What we don't realize now is that back then they used the train as we use the plane today. We don't think our story is typical of the time, but again it was not unusual.

Elbert Roscoe Gilbert was born on September 13, 1879, in Mooresboro, North Carolina. He was a twin, the youngest by a few minutes, and joined a family with four other siblings. His father was a country doctor, William W. Gilbert, and his mother was Margaret Maria Hollar. Elbert wanted to follow in his father's footsteps, but Dr. Gilbert thought that Elbert was not strong enough to lead the life of a country doctor.

He tried a number of different jobs after graduation from Ridge Academy in Vale, North Carolina, one of them as a potter in Jugtown. However, he eventually became a telegraph operator and found work in Asheville, Knoxville and Atlanta. You might say that he fell in love with long distance. At one time, he held down the main telegraph line from Atlanta to New York.

Moving from telegraphy to railroading, he became a conductor and traveled west. On one of his trips he met Bessie Isabel Hall in Salt Lake City, Utah. She was the daughter of Charles A. Hall, a dairy farmer and Mormon, and Sarah Larue, who were married in 1881 and started moving west from Illinois. Then they traveled to Missouri, Texas, Colorado and finally Salt Lake City. As Elbert was a Presbyterian, it must have been a difficult courtship, especially with his traveling back and forth from east to west. Bessie was known to have a good voice and sang in the Mormon Tabernacle Choir. Courting back then in Salt Lake City included taking the trolley from downtown out to Salt Air, a dance pavilion on the edge of the Great Salt Lake. Love apparently conquered all, and the couple was

Elbert Roscoe Gilbert and Bessie Isabel.

married in 1908. Bessie was almost nineteen. They spent their honeymoon in Eldorado Springs, Colorado, at a ranch owned by Elbert's uncle, Alexander Curtis.

Elbert had enrolled at Atlanta Dental College before that last trip to Salt Lake City. So Bessie and Elbert traveled east for the first time to live with Elbert's parents in Hickory, North Carolina. The summer before the fall semester found them operating a lunch stop outside Hickory on the Catawba River. Once enrolled, Elbert and several other students found that they were deficient in chemistry and so added to their regular course load by attending classes at Georgia Tech. Meanwhile, Bessie continued to live with her in-laws in Hickory while Elbert continued his studies. She would take the train to Atlanta from time to time to visit Elbert but could not afford to live there.

In the fall of 1911, Elbert had returned from Hickory to start the new semester. He couldn't find a room, and he told Bessie of his predicament. Two weeks later she arrived, found rooms on Williams Street and put her mind to helping Elbert. She became an early working wife to help put Elbert through school. She worked as a librarian at the college, as well as kept and boarded other students to help pay Elbert's tuition.

Marriage brought another Gilbert into the world when a daughter, Margaret Sarah, was born in February 1912. Elbert's age, a heavy class load and the increased responsibility of a newborn child did not keep Elbert from becoming president of his class and graduating with honors in 1913 at the age of thirty-four. After graduation, the family moved back to Hickory and set up his dental practice in nearby Henry, North Carolina. His background and high achievements at Atlanta Dental College had attracted the city fathers of Westminster, South Carolina, who invited him to practice there. So again they boarded the trains and moved to Westminster. They became involved with the Red Cross, Masonic Lodge, Eastern Star and the Presbyterian church.

Bessie and Margaret returned to visit some of her family in the west in 1915. They visited Bessie's sister, who had a candy shop that made its own candy in Kansas City, Missouri. Elbert came out for a visit, and she tried to convince him that he should open up a practice in Kansas City. Elbert apparently refused and returned to Westminster. However, early in 1916, he sold his practice and returned to Kansas City and opened up an office there. This lasted for about a year, and then he is reported to have said, "Bessie, I don't know about you and Margaret but I'm going back to Westminster." A crisis point had been reached in their marriage. According to Bessie, she would have liked to stay in Kansas City. She really didn't care for the South. But her love for Elbert was greater than anything. So they returned to Westminster where, once again, Elbert set up a dental practice.

Illness struck Elbert in 1918 when he contracted typhoid fever and Bright's disease. He was so sick that he was sent to Atlanta for treatment in a railroad boxcar on a cot with his doctor. He recovered but was so debilitated that he was forced to give up his dental practice. In January 1919, he was advised to move to a drier climate. He applied for a position as telegrapher with the San Pedro, Los Angeles and Salt Lake Railroad. He was offered a job as station agent and telegrapher with the railroad in Sage, Wyoming. It was there that Bessie learned Morse code and became a part-time telegraph operator to help Elbert. They lived in what looked like a railroad boxcar but was fitted out as a crew car with kitchen, living area and sleeping rooms. Little Margaret got her first dog and was happy out on the prairie.

It was two years before Elbert felt well enough to return to practicing dentistry. In 1921, Bessie, Elbert and little Margaret Sarah returned to Westminster. In addition to his dental practice, he managed the movie theatre in the building where he had his office. In the summer of 1922, the family went on a camping trip up to Highlands and lived on the side of Mirror Lake near the dam in a tent. They met Miss Margaret Harry, a Delano nurse, and she persuaded Elbert to come back to Highlands for several months the next summer to practice dentistry. He set up a portable dental chair at High Hampton in 1922. Of course, back then there was no electricity. He had a foot treadle drill and other supplies, including those to make dentures. In the summer of 1923, the family returned to Highlands and boarded at the Central House, and in 1924, they moved to Highlands, built a home on Mirror Lake and set up a full-time dental practice over Charlie Anderson's drugstore, which is now Mirror Lake Antiques.

Everything seemed well, but in 1926 Elbert suffered a serious illness that forced him to give up his dental practice again. The family decided to sell the house on Mirror Lake and rent the Richert home on Cashiers Road. Searching for another way to support his family, he embarked on a business career. He purchased an existing hardware business and hired Tudor N. Hall to manage it.

One of the stories told about Elbert and the hardware store concerned a gallon of paint. When one customer asked for a gallon of paint, Elbert took the can off the shelf and said, "That will be $2.25."

The customer replied, "I can get it for $1.75 from Sears."

"All right. You can have it for the Sears price."

The customer felt smug in getting the price down and handed Elbert the money. But Elbert put the can of paint back on the shelf.

"Wait, I paid for the paint. What are you doing?"

Elbert sighed, "Now I've sold you the paint at the Sears price. Right?"

"Yes, that's right. But why can't I get the paint?"

"How long would it take to get your paint from Sears?" Elbert asked.

"About two weeks, I guess."

"All right, come back in two weeks and you can have your paint."

Of course, the customer got his paint that day at the regular price.

It was not long before Bessie and Elbert's daughter, Margaret, fell in love with the store manager, Tudor, and they were married in 1928. Elbert returned to his dental practice on a part-time basis. He had many hobbies, including hunting and fishing. He was a founding member and president of what became known as Pierson's fish camp down on the Chatooga River in Whiteside Cove. He raised pheasants, enjoyed playing golf on the Hall House golf course and tended to the Civilian Conservation Corps (CCC) boys' dental needs back when their camp was located in Horse Cove. Tudor and Margaret had three children by 1932, and the two families decided to build a house on Fifth Street, which was part of the Hall House property.

The Presbyterian church was closed at this time. Bessie and several other wives went around to the past members of the church to help get it reopened. In 1929, the church was reopened with Elbert, Bessie and Margaret as charter members. Elbert was elected an Elder, and Bessie was president of the Women's Auxiliary. The Episcopal church was closed at this time.

Elbert's continuing health problems finally returned, and this time he succumbed on November 2, 1936. Bessie was now a widow at the young age of forty-seven. But she elected to stay with Margaret, Tudor and their family in the home they had all built together. She sold Elbert's practice to Jessie Zachary Moreland. With Elbert gone, she joined the Episcopal church, taught Sunday school, was head of the ECW (Episcopal Church Women), the first president of the newly formed Highlands Community Club and the president of the Hudson Library Association, taught children with learning disabilities at Highlands School, sang in the Presbyterian choir and later the Episcopal choir and was a chief instigator to have the twelfth grade added to the Highlands School. Between the church and helping with her three grandchildren, her life was full. She remained active in the community until the late 1960s and passed away in 1975. Dr. Herbert Koepp-Baker, retired Episcopal priest and member of the family, gave the eulogy at Bessie's funeral:

> *"Once when we talked alone of many things that affected both of us and our families," she said in her quiet and thoughtful way, "I hope that I may be remembered for what I have tried to be—what I have tried to do—and less for what I have said." This was the heart of the matter for her. Her family more and more grew to be an extension of herself and the center of her existence.*

So here we have a couple and later a family that traveled back and forth across the country much as we do today: holding down many jobs, living in various places and making the best of what life offered.

Their grandchildren called Bessie and Elbert "Dama" and "Docky." Her great-grandchildren called her G.G.

We have had a number of questions about how we get our material for these articles. Of course, it helps to have one of us whose roots go back to the 1820s. But we do research even with that background. For example, in this story we had postcards from the principals dating back to the early 1900s, photographs, Charles Hall's diary, information about Charles Hall's ancestry and family from the Church of Latter-Day Saints website www.familysearch.org, the 1880 census record of Dr. William Gilbert and his family from www.ancestry.com, personal oral history, copies of a biography by Margaret Gilbert Hall, a copy of the eulogy given by Dr. Koepp-Baker and church records. Now, if you want your grandchildren to know about their past, you can start assembling information. Keep those old letters and pictures (put names on the back) and talk to your parents and grandparents. Even if you aren't interested in your roots, someone down the line may want to know someday.

HENRY OSSAWA TANNER

There was a cool breeze coming up from the valley below. Clouds hung over the range of mountains and covered the far peaks in the distance. From the thick rhododendron growth, a horse and rider emerged near the top of Satulah Mountain. The rider dismounted his horse, tied the horse to a bent, stunted pine tree and then unstrapped a worn leather valise from the pommel of the saddle.

Looking around for a suitable place, he selected a flat spot covered with coarse grass near the edge of the solid granite ridge. He looked at his surroundings that were covered with a variety of native shrubs and low ground cover. Underneath the bent, windswept pines there was a patch of galax protected by low-growing rhododendron. As he opened the valise, an updraft of wind from below almost tore a pad of drawing paper from his hands. He was unfamiliar with the area and decided to move his position farther back from the edge. Finally settled, he removed a small wood campstool from the valise and then set several palettes of primary colors on a flat rock next to the pad of paper and small water flask. After sitting down on the campstool, he scanned the view from his position. Now he was ready.

The colors and clouds in the sky were continuously changing, and he noticed small fluffs of clouds in the valleys below. There were a number of peaks in the distance, some with sheer granite cliffs on one side and others completely covered in trees. He began painting, selecting the various colors, mixing them and then applying them to the top sheet of his drawing pad. Over the next few hours, he tried several techniques, from dry brush to wet

Henry Ossawa Tanner.

brush. Finally, he had half a dozen sketches and seemed satisfied with his work. He packed up all his materials in the valise, tied that to the saddle and carefully mounted his horse.

This could have been how Henry Ossawa Tanner painted a view from one of our mountaintops on the Highlands Plateau back in the summer of 1889. All that is known about his trip to Highlands was that it was for health reasons. One of the watercolor studies he made in Highlands is now at the National Museum of Art in Washington, D.C. It is titled *Highlands, North Carolina*. The painting here was done in oil and presumably from the watercolor studies. It had been titled for some time *Cumberland Foothills*, but at some point it was compared to the study in the museum in Washington and the title changed.

Henry Ossawa Tanner was born in Pittsburgh, Pennsylvania, on June 21, 1859. He was the son of Benjamin Tucker Tanner and Sarah Miller Tanner. Benjamin was a freedman, but Sarah was born a slave in Virginia. Later she and her brothers and sisters escaped to Pennsylvania via the Underground Railroad. They were married in 1858, and Henry was their first child. Benjamin graduated from Avery College and later from Western

A Highlands painting, by Henry Ossawa Tanner.

Theological Seminary. He was ordained in the African Methodist Episcopal Church in 1860.

Henry's middle name was taken from the village of Osawatomie, Kansas, where John Brown began his antislavery campaign in 1856. The family moved to Washington, D.C., before Lincoln was inaugurated president but later returned to Pittsburgh. In 1872, they moved again, this time to Philadelphia where Henry and his brothers and sisters were raised. Benjamin Tanner had planned on his son going into the ministry, but Henry had different ideas. In 1879, he enrolled in the Pennsylvania Academy of Fine Arts. He had decided that he would become a famous American marine painter, as there were very few in this field. Later on, he changed his mind to becoming a famous painter of animals, again because the field was wide open. At the academy his work was judged to be very good, but racial discrimination tested him, and his fellow white students hazed him. After graduation, he worked hard as a commercial artist primarily by doing magazine illustrations.

In January 1889, he left his home in Philadelphia and moved to Atlanta, Georgia, where he opened a photography studio. That fall, after his photography studio failed, Bishop Hartzell of the Methodist Episcopal Church sponsored him for a position at Clark University in Atlanta. But in 1891 he made the move that would change his life. On a trip to Rome by way of London and Paris, he decided to stay in Paris and enroll in the Academie Julian founded in 1868 by Rodolph Julian as a private studio school for art students. He returned to America in 1893 to recuperate from typhoid fever but returned to Paris the following year. In 1896, he received an honorable mention at the Salon in Paris, his first award. In 1897 his painting, *The Resurrection of Lazarus*, was purchased by the French government, along with a painting by John Singer Sergeant, and hung in the Luxembourg Gallery. For the remainder of the 1890s, Tanner traveled a great deal. In 1898, he met Jessie Macauley Olsen from San Francisco. They were married the following year, and she became the model for many of his paintings.

By the turn of the century, Tanner's works were being exhibited throughout cities in the eastern United States, as well as in France. In addition, he was serving on art juries on both sides of the Atlantic. Tanner's works run the gamut from paintings of horses to depictions of Mary Magdalene.

From time to time, he created works inspired by African Americans, the most notable being *The Banjo Lesson*. Working in Paris, where Negroes were accepted, he and his art thrived. He, like Josephine Baker and a number of other Negroes, came to France to escape racial discrimination. Had he remained in the United States, he probably would not have received the international recognition that came to him.

He volunteered and served in the American Red Cross during World War I. One of his paintings of that period, *American Red Cross Canteen*, hangs in the American Red Cross headquarters in Washington, D.C. Tanner's paintings now hang in many of the major galleries and museums of the United States, as well as in western Europe. There are a great number in private collections. Tanner died in 1937.

Information for this article came from a video produced by Tanner Film Group and can be located in the Macon County Library. Another great source was the book Henry Ossawa Tanner, *produced by the Philadelphia Museum of Art.*

We want to thank Thomas Styron, director of the Greenville Museum of Art and part-time Highlands resident, for bringing Henry Ossawa Tanner to our attention. We also want to thank Robert Boyce and the Berea College Art Department for permission to use a photo of the Highlands painting. Finally, thanks to Rosemary Stiefel for help and advice on the materials and techniques Tanner may have used here in Highlands. When this originally appeared in the Laurel *magazine, we asked if anyone could identify the setting for the painting. We received a letter and a photograph from Mike Thompson. The photograph was taken from the spot where Tanner's painting was made. The mountains in the foreground and background match exactly.*

THOMAS FLEMING PARKER

Remember that television series that began, "There are eight million stories in this city"? Well, there are a lot of different stories about how people came to Highlands, their impact on our town and what kind of persons they were. This is one of the lesser-known stories and concerns an impact not only on our town but also parts of South Carolina.

On James Island, near Charleston, South Carolina, there is the small town of Secessionville. Before the Civil War, it was a summer resort for the island planters. There were three regiments of Confederate troops stationed nearby on the morning of June 16, 1862, when nine regiments of Union troops planned a surprise attack on the Confederate battery. It was a hard-fought battle with bravery shown on both sides. Outnumbered perhaps three or four to one, the Confederates had the advantage of marshes guarding both of their flanks. This limited the number of Union regiments that could be brought to bear. The outcome was lopsided: 1,604 Union soldiers either killed, wounded or captured to 48 Confederate killed and 106 wounded.

The battle began shortly after 4:00 a.m. and was over by 9:00 a.m. Thomas Parker was on patrol when the attack began. He was one of the first on the parapet to fall.

If Thomas Fleming Parker had not lost his father, Thomas Parker, in the Civil War, we might never have heard of him at all. Thomas F. Parker was born in 1860. His mother was Margaretta Amelia Fleming of Charleston, South Carolina. When the war came, Tom's father enlisted. He was a successful merchant with the firm of Robert Adger & Co., and his friends advised him to buy a substitute. His obituary quotes him, "I scorn to buy a substitute." He left his widow Margaretta, a daughter Clarissa Anne Fleming and son Thomas Fleming. Tragically, Clarissa died of diphtheria just five months later.

The war took a great toll on many Southern families. Margaretta and her only son were one of those families who had suffered the loss of a father, husband or brother. Margaretta's parents, Thomas and Clarissa Walton Fleming, though well-to-do before the war, lost their fortunes after. In 1865, Margaretta married Captain Samuel Prioleau Ravenel, another

Thomas Fleming Parker.

Charlestonian. Earlier that year, he had come to the Highlands Plateau to buy land for his fiancée, Margaretta, and himself. He had visited the area before the war and had fallen in love with it. Captain Ravenel adopted young Thomas Fleming Parker and raised him as his own. The couple went on to have a son, Samuel P. Ravenel Jr., and three daughters, Marguerite, Clarissa "Clair" Amelia and Caroline Elise. Young Thomas attended the College of Charleston, as had his father, but was forced to drop out due to eye problems.

Meanwhile, Margaretta and Prioleau returned to Highlands, now a new town, and built a home on Wolf Ridge. They called it Wantoot after the early Ravenel plantation outside of Charleston. From their front porch, Margaretta said she could see her home in Pendleton, South Carolina. By this time, Prioleau had bought much of the land between Satulah and Cashiers. Several years later, Margaretta bought the Skinner home in town and renamed it Islington House. In 1884, Prioleau and Thomas Parker came to Highlands and supervised the construction of the First Presbyterian Church. Margaretta and her sister, Clair Fleming Burt, had donated $3,000 for the building of the new church. Thomas designed the pews and the first altar for the church. Later, in the late 1880s, Thomas worked with S.T. Kelsey and his son Harlan at the nursery that Kelsey had started shortly after founding the town. In 1887, he married Lisa deVeaux Foulke from Philadelphia. She died in Greenville in 1902.

In 1890, the Kelseys left to begin a new town in North Carolina that they called Linville. After several attempts to attract a financial partner, Prioleau Ravenel came forward. While the Kelseys were working on the development of Linville, they turned over the management of the nursery in Highlands to Thomas Parker.

By the late 1890s, Parker had gone to Philadelphia and in 1899 moved to Greenville, South Carolina. He opened the Monaghan Mill, a textile manufacturing company. He ran this for twelve years and continued on as vice-president of the Parker Mill when it merged with Monaghan Mill. Monaghan was outside of Greenville and was basically raw ground when he started it. He employed a landscape architect to lay out the property with employee homes, playgrounds and a cemetery.

Later in Greenville, Parker was responsible for, or was a major instigator of, many of the civic changes to the city, including the construction of the Salvation Army Hospital, the Greenville County Library, the YMCA and the Phyllis Wheatley Center. He even remembered his old friend Harlan P. Kelsey, who by now had a nursery in Boxford, Massachusetts. Parker brought Kelsey to Greenville to give a report that initiated city planning. His greatest achievement, though, was thought to be the establishment of the library.

In 1902, his stepfather and good friend Prioleau Ravenel died. In 1906, Parker remarried Harriet Horry Frost from Charleston, South Carolina. Following this, in 1913, his mother died. But he was very close to his two half sisters, Marguerite and Clarissa, both of whom had remained single. They sold Wantoot to the Monroe family from New Orleans in 1914 and moved up the ridge to build a new Ravenel home, Wolf Ridge. Parker built the home while keeping busy in the mill business in Greenville.

Thomas Fleming Parker died in 1926. He left two children by his first wife—Thomas Fleming Parker and Julia deVeaux Parker—and Thomas Parker by his second wife. A grandson of Thomas F. Parker, Joseph F. Parker, lives in Whiteside Cove in Highlands. Joe tells us that he got his property by way of his grandfather in an unusual way. It seems his grandfather was a member of the Outers Club, sometimes called "Monroe's Fish Camp," but had a falling out with the other members and was "kicked out." Parker retaliated by buying the land leading up to the club/camp; the subject of one of our earlier biographies, Elbert Gilbert, was also a member of this group.

We want to thank Joe Parker for the many materials and Parker family genealogy, as well as the picture of his great-grandfather.

REVEREND A. RUFUS MORGAN, 1885–1983

It is possible to believe that you know someone fairly well and then find out that you have only scratched the surface of his or her life. That is what I found out when Isabel suggested that we write about one of our church's former ministers. Isabel had known him longer than I; after all she was a cradle Episcopalian. I had picked up information from time to time, but I still didn't know the man.

The gentleman answered to a number of salutations: Mr. Morgan, Dr. Morgan, A. Rufus, or, in later years, "Uncle Rufus" but never Father Morgan. Isabel first knew him as a child. He was her priest. I got to know him later as a teenager when attending church functions with Isabel. By that time, A. Rufus had already accomplished more than most men or women do in a lifetime. I had no idea of what kind of man he had been or what he had done. I thought he was an elderly gentleman that had found a home in the priesthood and was content with a quiet life.

A. Rufus was priest-in-charge for the Church of Incarnation when Isabel and I decided to get married. At that time, it was a mission, along with a number of other churches in Western North Carolina. Dr. Morgan looked after many of them. We would like to tell you something of the life of this quiet but dedicated priest.

According to his autobiography, he was born in a log cabin "in the shadow of the Nantahala Mountains," the oldest son and one of nine children, of which six survived to adulthood. Hard work, long hours and very little chance for an education faced him as a young man. His father was a farmer and looked to his sons, as any farmer would, to help on the farm. He first attended a one-room school and then schools in other communities after the family had moved from the Cartoogechaye Valley to Murphy, North Carolina. His mother's religious convictions were a great influence on him and his brothers and sisters. She was a strong believer in the Anglican faith. The family reading ran from Shakespeare to the Bible. After completing the highest grade in the Murphy schools, Rufus asked his father's permission to move to where he could continue his education through high school. This was a hard question for his father, but he accepted Rufus's wishes.

Reverend A. Rufus Morgan.

From Waynesville High School, he was accepted at Chapel Hill and eventually to divinity school in New York at General Theological Seminary. He rounded out his formal education at Columbia University. He did all of this on his own with jobs from janitor to deacon at St. Peter's in New York.

After graduation, but while he was pursuing a PhD, he met and married Madeline Prentiss from Fall River, Massachusetts. She was tutoring him in German. His marriage brought an end to his plans for a PhD. They returned to Western North Carolina and the small town of Penland, where, with the help of his sister Lucy Morgan, he started the Appalachian Industrial School. Help from friends he had known in New York enabled him to erect the first building. Lucy continued her work there, which she made famous as the Penland School of Weaving and Pottery. In addition to the school, the bishop also gave A. Rufus the task of establishing the church in Yancey, Mitchell and Avery Counties. This was the beginning of his missionary work that would take him to the Diocese of Upper South Carolina in 1918. By then, he and Madeline had two children, Kathryn and Rufus Jr. They stayed in that diocese and ministered to many parishes, and he ended up as rector of St. John's in Columbia. He then accepted a call from Bishop Gribben of the Diocese of Western North Carolina to return home to his beloved Cartoogechaye Valley in 1940.

A. Rufus was now fifty-five years old and could have been thinking about retirement. Instead, he took on the job to establish and carry on the missionary work of Reverend John A. Deal, who had married his parents, Alfred Morgan and Fanny Siler, back in 1881. Reverend Deal had started many of the missions west of Asheville.

A. Rufus lived in Franklin until 1951, when he returned to his family's homestead, called Nonah. Although he had a number of missions to minister to, he was back in his beloved mountains. He had been a hiker, and now he turned his attention to the Appalachian Trail, which passed nearby. At one time, he maintained almost fifty miles of the trail by himself or with the help of Boy Scouts. A group of men saw the need to continue the trail maintenance, and the Nantahala Hiking Club was formed. They would meet at Nonah.

A. Rufus first climbed Mount LeConte before the formation of the Great Smoky Mountain National Park. He climbed once almost every year and sometimes more until his ninety-second birthday. In later years, when he was totally blind, he continued the trek up the mountain and seemed to sense the native plants, which he pointed out to his friends. Isabel and I have made that climb and can appreciate the effort it must have been for him. Georgia Public Television made a documentary of one of those last hikes.

There is so much to tell of this man: his love for the mountains and the rare and hard-to-find species of various plants and his concern for those less fortunate and all that he did during his active life to help them.

A. Rufus's story of rebuilding the church at Cartoogechaye is an example of what one man can do. The old church, St. John's, was built on land given by his grandfather. It was abandoned by the diocese when it was thought that the small country churches should be consolidated. That structure fell into disrepair, and only the graveyard was left. Many of the graves were moved to Franklin, but some of the gravestones remained. When A. Rufus returned to North Carolina, he decided that the church should be rebuilt. That was 1940. So he had white pines in the churchyard cut down, sawn into lumber and dried, and this became the paneling for the interior of the church. He secured logs from the U.S. Forest Service, which were then turned into framing and siding. He asked his relatives for permission to use the old tombstones to form the foundation. Friends gave money, time and talent to build the church. It was finished in 1945. Upon hearing of the new church, then Bishop Gribben asked how much of a debt was owed. The bishop was relieved to hear that there was no debt. Later in 1948, Bishop M. George Henry consecrated the church.

A fire destroyed his beloved Nonah in 1975. A. Rufus was ninety that year. He lost all his collections, books, records and other items accumulated over the years. Friends and his daughter and son-in-law came to his aid and soon rebuilt the home. Part of it is an old log cabin and chimney.

A. Rufus began writing poetry at some point and had the poems printed on postcards to send to friends at Christmas. Originally, a collection of these poems was printed in a booklet *Radiant Light*. It went into a second edition in 1974. Copies of *Radiant Light II* can be found in the Hudson Library. His autobiography, *From Cabin to Cabin*, can be found at St. John's Cartoogechaye. Proceeds from its sales go to help support St. Johns. There is also a booklet, *History of St. John's Episcopal Church: Macon County North Carolina*. So what can you say about a man whose life has been dedicated to others? Thank you, A. Rufus!

We were fortunate to know both A. Rufus and Bishop Henry. They conducted our wedding service. *Later, while A. Rufus was still our priest in Highlands before retiring, Isabel played the organ for Sunday services and I became a lay reader. I and several others would conduct morning prayer when A. Rufus was serving at other missions.*

THE ROOTS OF HIGHLANDS

A black Chevrolet pulled up in front of a house near the corner of Main and Third Streets. The driver, a white-haired lady with a kind smile, got out and went up to the porch of the house and let herself in. She looked around the living room filled with Chinese curios, Italian ceramics and odd pieces of furniture. There were two women, one the visitor's age and another somewhat younger, sitting in front of the fireplace.

"Good morning, Mrs. Root. It's a beautiful day isn't it?" The visitor greeted the older woman.

Addie Root got up from her chair. "Yes, Mrs. Porterfield. It's nice to see you. Is there something in particular I can help you with?"

"Why, yes. I'm looking for a wedding present. Maybe some silver."

"Well, that's a coincidence. I received some Sheffield plate last week." She led Mrs. Porterfield back to the dining room where she displayed most of her silver. "Let's see. What do you think about a serving spoon? Here's a pair of them."

"That will be just right. The wedding is the middle of June, at the Episcopal church here in town. But I wanted to buy the present now and take it over to the house. Could you wrap them up for me?"

The Root family. Joseph E. Root is in the front row, second from right, and Addie is in the middle row, also second from right. *Courtesy of Mary Elizabeth Cone.*

"Yes indeed. Would you like a cup of tea while you're waiting? I can ask one of the girls to bring one from next door."

"No thank you. I've got some other errands to run: the post office and Potts' grocery. I'll just sit down."

Mrs. Root picked up the spoons and took them into the kitchen. That was her wrapping room during business hours.

Mrs. Porterfield looked around the house again. It was hard to imagine how Addie and Ed Root had lived in this house for almost twenty years. There were gifts all over the living room, dining room and in the two other rooms. One room had rugs, and behind it, off the dining room, there were tables and shelves with hand-woven placemats and throws from Churchill Weavers and the weavers over in Norton. In the corner there was a cabinet with doll dresses and dollhouse furniture. Over on the left Alice Inman had her sweater shop in what was not much more than an alcove. Alice carried Pringle sweater sets, cashmere sweaters and knitting yarn. Mrs. Porterfield remembered that back during the war Alice had taught many of the girls and women of Highlands to knit. Some only got as far as knitting the squares that someone else sewed together to make those throws that were sent overseas to the soldiers. But others learned how to make sweaters and socks.

"Here you are Mrs. Porterfield. I put the spoons in tissue paper so they won't rattle. Is it Isabel Hall's wedding that these are for?"

"How did you guess that?"

"Well, we've had a lot of folks in looking for wedding gifts, and that's the only wedding besides Horner Stockton's daughter, you know that lawyer from Franklin. If I don't see you sooner, I'll see you at the wedding."

Joseph E. Root and his wife Addie arrived in Highlands in 1925. Mr. Root, known by his family as Ed, was a civil engineer by training and education. They had come to Highlands from Crawford, Kansas, as Ed was involved in the new city water plant construction, the first one for the town. They bought their first piece of property down on Bruner Lane. After the water plant was completed, Ed and Addie decided to stay. The town was growing, and Ed's training as a surveyor and professional engineer was very much in need. In 1933, they purchased a number of lots on Main Street, starting at the corner of Third, where Reeves Hardware is now located. They also purchased other downtown property. What came next was a fluke of circumstances that neither of them planned.

A close friend from South Carolina, Mrs. N. Gist Gee, sent Addie several boxes of things that she had picked up in China, which she thought Mrs. Root could sell. When the boxes arrived, she set them on the floor behind the front door. As the story goes, one of her friends brought some summer residents by. Addie had not had time to open the boxes before that time. She was as amazed as her friend and guests were when they did open the boxes. They were full of an interesting collection of handmade Chinese items: old porcelain, quilts, embroidered linen and quite a bit more. When asked what she was going to do with them, Addie had no answer. First one and then another of the women asked if she could buy something. And so Root's Gift Shop was born. As far as we know, it was the first true gift shop in Highlands. It was later that Fraser Redden opened his High Hills Jam Pot and Mrs. Young opened Wit's End.

She continued to receive items from her friend Mrs. Gee until the war in China curtailed that source. She began, like any other gift shop owner, to make trips to the New York gift markets. Gradually, the stock began to take up more and more of the home, at least during the summer season. After the founding of the Southern Highland Handicraft Guild in the mid-1930s, she started adding handmade items to her inventory. The Highlands-Cashiers area was a treasure-trove of craftsmen and craftswomen making handmade baskets and chairs, weaving and creating other handmade crafts. Until the early 1940s, she had no competition from other shops in town. She even branched out into mail order—that is, she was happy to take orders from people who had visited in the summer and called or wrote for gifts.

Later, the Roots added a second business, the Highlands Tea Room, which was located in a small building at the very corner of Third and Main Streets. The Tea Room was famous for its homemade cakes, pies and ham sandwiches. The Roots baked their own hams. There were a number of teenage girls that worked there. At one time, three Hicks sisters including Grace Hicks Zoellner, Vellamae Hicks Potts and Alvina Hicks Bowers were there, as well as Betty Potts Little. Alvina remembers working there in the summer. They would come to work at seven o'clock and stay until the last customer was served. A lot of their customers would come in later in the evening after cocktail parties. They offered a choice of two meats and vegetables for fifty cents. A peanut butter sandwich was a dime, and when you added jelly it was fifteen cents. Later, they used to serve sandwiches to the folks who rode the open-topped touring buses that came through town.

We haven't told you too much about Mr. Root. Even before the Highlands Country Club opened, Mr. Root was the chief engineer for the golf course. Later, Mr. Happoldt made Mr. Root his head surveyor. As Charlie McDowell remembers, Mr. Root was from the old school of surveying—slope surveying rather than horizontal surveying. Before Mr. Root retired from surveying, he took Charlie around the club and showed him several lots that he had done. He explained to Charlie that his bearing and distances may differ from a horizontal survey, but his corners would be the same. If you don't understand this, just ask Charlie to explain it.

After Mrs. Root died in 1961, Mr. Root closed the shop and Tea Room. He later became friends with the new owner of the Phelps House across the street, Evona Phelps. She was a younger sister of Milida Phelps Thurman. Evona was the new owner of the Phelps House, but it was her sister Milida who ran the restaurant. Later Mr. Root sold his Main Street property to Evona Phelps. Mr. Root passed away in 1967. We believe that Mrs. Root was buried in Charlotte. If anyone knows where Mr. Root is buried, we would appreciate finding out. We think the Roots would make a great addition to the Highlands Historical Society's annual "Walk in the Park."

Mrs. Root had a son by the name of Roy, who was living with them in Crawford, Kansas, in 1920.

We would like to thank Wilson and Mary Elizabeth Cone and their daughter, Patricia Cone, for their information about the Roots. Mrs. Cone is the niece and Patricia the grandniece of Addie Root. Mrs. Cone remembers visiting the Roots with her mother, Addie Root's sister, and helping in the shop during the summer. They also gave us a copy of an article about the Roots, which appeared in the Christian Science Monitor *in 1957. Also thanks to Charlie McDowell, Chuck Crane, Alvina Hicks Bowers and Betty Potts Little for their help in writing this article.*

THE WEAVERS OF NORTON

Weaving in our mountains was a matter of necessity in the early days of the country. Communities were separated by a lack of roads, hard money was in short supply or nonexistent and families had to be self-sufficient. Store-bought clothes were literally beyond the reach of most people who lived in the hills and coves of the Appalachians. It was up to the women of the household—mothers, grannies and daughters all participated in the process of making clothes, bed covers, rugs and anything else that required cloth. The looms were big, cumbersome and took up so much room that they were usually kept on the porch. The raw material was from sheep on the hoof, either in a fenced pasture or roaming the hills and woods around the homeplace.

From what the old-timers told the students of Rabun Gap School when they were researching for their book *Foxfire II*, sheepdogs were not used. Minnie Buchanan was quoted as saying, "Once in a while there was an old shepherd dog that would kill 'em." They all agreed that their parents used the two-legged variety, their children, as sheepdogs. Just reading the description of the long process from shearing the sheep to the finished product of a coverlet or rug makes one appreciate this craft and art. After the wool was gathered, it was washed, sometimes twice, first in warm water with some type of detergent and then rinsed in cold water. Next it was carded to separate the fibers and then wrapped around a corn shuck that was slipped over the spindle of the spinning wheel and spun into thread on a bobbin. Some bobbins were made of stems of doghobble. This was a job that many of those interviewed enjoyed even to the point of carding and spinning late into the night. We guess it was relaxing in a way. A time to let your mind wander while your body followed an age-old theme handed down from mother to daughter over generations.

Plain stuff was woven from the natural wool, but for any material that required color, it was necessary to gather natural roots, bark, flowers and nuts to make the different colors. This was a chore for young and old alike. Peggy Rowbottom remembers going into the fields and woods with her

Left to right: Minnie Buchanan, Henry and Dorothy Conkle of the Carolina Mountain Shop and Lula Norton. *Courtesy of Lassie Buchanan.*

Aunt Lula to gather yellow root (yellow wood) and doghobble (*Leucothoe*). Many other plants were used including coreopsis, gray moss, walnut hulls and roots, straw and madder. The raw plant matter would then be boiled in an iron pot with the wool and some type of mordant, a fixative, to fix the color from fading later. This was usually vinegar or salt, but for certain plant matter copperas, a green sulfate of iron, alum and other mordants, was used. Acetic acid was used to color red and potassium dichromate to color yellow. Walnut hulls didn't require a mordant since the brown color rarely faded. Lula Norton's method was to boil walnut hulls until they became mushy. Then she strained the dye and put the skeins of wool into it. This dye could go from a tan to brown. Minnie Buchanan's recipe was to put two gallons of walnut hulls in a cloth sack, add water and the wool in an iron pot and boil the water for an hour.

Finally, the dyed skeins of wool could be taken to the loom and a rug, coverlet or material for some type of clothing could be made. It was a long, time-consuming process but one that could be started and finished in a day.

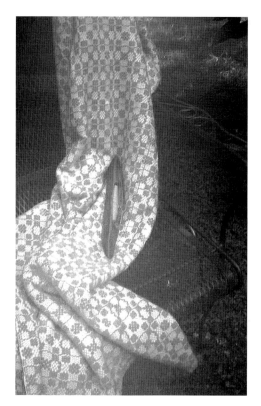

Woven coverlet by Minnie Buchanan, given to her granddaughter Carol Jane Buchanan. The pattern was handed down from English ancestors. The wood shuttle and bobbin were made from doghobble. *Courtesy of Carol Jane Buchannan.*

So as the hills opened up with roads, stores began carrying clothing and hard money from crops and jobs became available. The sheep were no longer needed, and the dye pot, loom and spinning wheel became antiquated and unnecessary. And the art of weaving almost died.

In the early 1920s, there was a revival of weaving in the Appalachian Mountains. Sponsors of this revival were various settlement schools, Pi Beta Phi sorority, Berea Academy and College and motivated individuals, Allanstand Craft Shop in Asheville, Arrowmont School, Appalachian School, Penland School and many others that contributed to the resurgence. Individuals like Lucy Morgan, Mary Hambidge and Bonnie Willis Ford are some of the better-known names who encouraged this return to hand weaving. In particular, there is still a Hambidge Center down near Betty's Creek in Rabun County, which was started by Mary Hambidge in the mid-1930s.

What has all this to do with Highlands and Cashiers, though? Descendants and relatives of Lula Evitt Norton and Minnie Gregory Buchanan could tell you. Over in the Norton community, between Highlands and Cashiers, Lula Norton began weaving and later taught other women in the community to weave to help bring in cash for their families. She opened a shop next to her home on Norton Road and called it the Dye Pot but later changed the name to Cabin Weavers. Lula did it all in the craft of weaving. She picked her own dye materials, carded, spun, dyed her yarn and set up the loom. She liked to set up a pattern and then register it with the Weaver's Guild. Other women that worked with Lula were Phoebe Price, Elsie Potts and Lola Fox.

Minnie bought the business from Lula and changed the name to Bucky's Handweaving. Her son, "Smokey," built the shop, which is still standing across Norton Road from Smokey and Lassie Buchanan's home. Their daughter, Carol Jane Buchanan, told me that as a child she would spend hours at the shop watching her "Granny" Buchanan weave and sometimes sit on her lap at the loom.

Minnie's husband, Jacob Daniel Buchanan, died in 1933 during the Great Depression. It was at that time that Minnie would walk from her home on Norton Road over the mountain to Pine Creek to work in a sewing shop. The round trip started in the dark of the morning and end in the dark of the night. According to her family, though, she did this and the weaving business later without one complaint. John Parris, noted columnist for the *Asheville Citizen Times*, recognized Minnie in this way when he autographed one of his books: "Minnie Buchanan is of my mountains and my people—as real and true to her heritage, as only an honest to goodness mountain woman can be."

The weaving of these women could be found in Henry and Dorothy Conkle's Carolina Mountain Shop in Cashiers, Mrs. Root's Gift Shop and Frazer Redden's High Hills Jam Pot in Highlands, as well as in Asheville, North Carolina.

As a side note to our article, Isabel is a third cousin of Lula Norton, and Tony remembers visiting Lula's store back in the late 1930s with his mother. Norton back then was a treasure of native craftspeople, including the weavers, basket makers and makers of handmade oak chairs with split-oak bottoms.

We want to thank Peggy Rowbottom, Lassie, Smokey, Carol Jane Buchanan and the young students from Rabun Gap-Nacoochee School who gathered and wrote the chapter in Foxfire II, *especially David and Carlton Young, who were neighbors of Lula and Minnie at that time. Also helpful were the articles in* Macon County History, *volume*

2, written by Carol Jane Buchanan, and Weavers of the Southern Highlands *by Philis Alvic. For more information on the weaving revival, we recommend* Gift from the Hills *by Lucy Morgan and Legette Blythe.*

A STORY OF TWO FORMER FOES: PART I

We would like to tell a story of two unlikely neighbors—you might say pioneers—of Highlands. Both of these men were born the same year, 1844. Both fought in the War Between the States, the Civil War, or as those born north of the Mason-Dixon line called it, the Rebellion. Their year of birth and the war they fought in were the only two things that these men had in common. So let's start with John H. Durgin.

John Durgin was born in West Campton, Grafton County, New Hampshire. His father, Charles, was a farmer and a native of New Hampshire; his mother, Eliza, was a native of North Carolina. That in itself would probably make a good story. At age sixteen, he was living at home in 1860, but two years later he had enlisted as a private in Company E of the Tenth New Hampshire Volunteer Infantry Regiment. He later was promoted to the rank of sergeant. John saw action in a number of major battles of the Civil War, including the Battle of Fredericksburg, the Siege of Suffolk, the Peninsular Campaign, Cold Harbor, Petersburg, the Battle of Fair Oaks and so on. By June 1865, the regiment had lost 7 officers and 54 enlisted men in battle and 1 officer and 133 enlisted men from disease. Luck or something else saw John through that terrible war. David Norton, Isabel's great-grandfather, was on the other side of the lines at Petersburg.

After the Confederate surrender at Appomattox Court House, the regiment was moved back to Manchester, New Hampshire, where he was mustered out. But John apparently had become accustomed to army life. He may have returned to his parents' farm in Campton, New Hampshire, but the following year he enlisted in the Seventh Cavalry Regiment and went west with Lieutenant Colonel George Armstrong Custer. His first action, in 1867, was against the southern Cheyenne. This proved to be an unsuccessful campaign. Later that year, Custer was court-martialed and suspended from duty for a year for being absent during part of the campaign. His old friend, General Phil Sheridan, accepted Custer's reasons and sent him back to duty. Custer, the regiment and John Durgin participated in a later battle in 1868 with Black Kettle's band near the Washita River. This engagement refurbished Custer's flagging reputation. By 1871, John had apparently had enough of the West and the army and returned to New England. He was twenty-seven years old and for the previous ten years had faced life-threatening danger.

Back east, John settled in the West Roxbury area of Boston and became a carpenter. In just a little over a year, he met and married Martha Ann Brown. Children soon followed, with Ella Bernice "Bernie" born in 1874, Frances W. "Fannie" in 1876 and Christine in 1878. The family remained in Boston until 1883, when they moved to Highlands. By then, John had contracted tuberculosis, and his doctors may have suggested the higher climate of our new town. He also could have read some of the pamphlets that were circulating throughout New England about our climate. Whatever the reason, John probably made the best decision of his life.

When the family arrived in Highlands, John purchased a three-acre parcel at the northeast corner of Fifth and Chestnut Streets, where they built their home. The Highlands' climate, a change of heart, a new lease on life—we'll never know what did it, but John Durgin survived. Later, when Dr. Mary Lapham opened her tuberculosis sanatorium in the early part of the twentieth century, Bernie became her nurse. Perhaps she saw to it that her father got some of the treatments that Dr. Lapham's patients received. Fannie died in 1900, and her mother died in 1921. We don't know what happened to Christine, but none of the girls ever married.

The man who survived disease and gunfire in the Civil War, campaigns against the Indians and finally tuberculosis outlived all of his family except Bernie. He passed away in 1939, and Bernie followed him the next year. Old-timers still refer to that area on Fifth and Chestnut Streets as Durgin's corner.

A STORY OF TWO FORMER FOES: PART II

We told you about John Durgin, Civil War veteran and scout for General George Armstrong Custer, and about his move to Highlands in 1883. His neighbor across Chestnut Street from 1896 to 1918 was Tudor Tucker Hall.

So let us tell you about T.T. Hall. We know somewhat more about his life than John Durgin's, as he was Isabel's grandfather. Her information about him comes primarily through her father, Tudor Norton Hall. T.T.

was born on December 6, 1844, in Darien, Georgia, so he was the same age as Durgin. T.T. was the son of Henry Tucker Hall, who was born in Bermuda in the mid-1790s, and Susan Marion Harrison, a native of Darien, McIntosh County, Georgia.

T.T. was born into a typical Southern planter–class family. His father owned slaves and probably raised indigo and/or cotton. He had a large number of brothers and sisters, plus several half brothers and sisters by his father's first wife, Sarah Gignilliat. After Sarah died, he remarried Susan Marion Harrison.

During the Civil War, a Massachusetts regiment burned the town of Darien to the ground. So most of the existing records are those either saved by individuals or Savannah newspaper articles. About 1849, the family moved to Decatur, Georgia, and later to Aiken, South Carolina.

During this period, T.T.'s father turned from planter to import-export merchant. He made frequent trips to Charleston, South Carolina, where he was associated with William P. Hall, a relative we believe. In June 1862, at age eighteen, he enlisted in Captain Matthews's heavy artillery battery,

Tudor Tucker Hall.

94

which was formed in Aiken. This unit was attached to the Fifteenth South Carolina Heavy Artillery Battalion in June 1863, with General P.G.T. Beauregard as overall commander of the defense of Charleston. We don't know what happened that first year, but archives show that the battery was part of the Confederate forces defending Morris Island near Charleston on July 1863. Some records show that the unit was involved in North Carolina late in the war, but they surrendered in April 1865.

T.T. survived the war and returned to Aiken and his family. By 1870, he was back in Charleston as a clerk for William P. Hall's import business. He met and married Harriet Dawson of Charleston and began to raise a family. Later, in the early 1880s, he took over the business with another clerk and the widow of William P. Hall. He and Harriet Dawson Hall had four children, two of whom survived infancy. The two survivors, Deas and Henry T. "Harry," are described elsewhere in this book.

We're not sure how T.T. and Harriet found out about Highlands. He was in good health at the time, but Harriet was not. There is a letter from Dr. Charles Frost to T.T. offering his home in Highlands for sale. The Halls may also have heard of Highlands from Prioleau and Margaretta Ravenel in Charleston. Dr. Frost had bought it unfinished from C.C. Hutchinson. So the Halls moved with their two children to Highlands in 1889. In the meantime, Dr. Frost and his second wife, Meta Norton, had built a new home on the north side of the same property. They called their new home Meadow House. The Halls and Frosts became good friends and visited one another often. Both families were attending Episcopal services in various homes in Highlands that were conducted by Reverend Archibald Deal. Their two families and others wished to build a church for regular worship.

Dr. Frost passed away in 1893, and Meta Norton Frost joined her father, David Norton, to help manage the Central House hotel. T.T.'s wife Harriet died that same year. T.T. and Meta, already close friends, began courting and were married at the Central House in 1896, the year that the Episcopal Church of the Incarnation was dedicated. They sold T.T.'s home on Main Street and moved to the Meadow House. It was located near the corner of Sixth and Chestnut Streets. Meta and T.T. started a summer resort, probably stemming from Meta's hotel experience helping her father at the Central House. They created a lake and built a nine-hole golf course, a dance pavilion and a clay tennis court and gradually enlarged the original home. Five children were added to the family between 1898 and 1910: Mattie, Jack, Dorothy, Tudor N. and Caroline. Meta would have been just forty-six when Caroline was born in 1910.

T.T. enjoyed both golf and skeet shooting, two sports in which he was active in Charleston. Their golf course was either the first or second one in Highlands, at least twenty-five years before Highlands Country Club. Since T.T. had competed in skeet shooting events in Charleston, he continued this sport on his golf course in Highlands.

As the first resort that we know of in Highlands, it attracted families that could actually spend their entire summer here. Early on, before the automobile became common, visitors would come by train to Walhalla or Seneca and be met by stages that would bring them up the mountain on a two-day journey. They would spend the night at Russell's, a regular coach stop between Walhalla and Highlands. Later, T.T. bought an automobile, which he never drove. Either Jack or Tudor, his two sons, would drive to Walhalla or Seneca and meet the trains. Tudor made his first trip when he was eleven years old. Some of the families that came to the Hall House later bought or built homes in Highlands. Occasionally, people have told Isabel that their parents or grandparents had stayed at the Hall House.

Tudor Tucker Hall passed away in 1918. He was seventy-four years old. His neighbor across the street, John Durgin, lived twenty-one more years and died in 1939 at age ninety-five. Meta continued on with the Hall House with the help of her children. Then she leased the Highlands telephone exchange, and some of the children ran that. A flood or hurricane washed out the dam for the lake, and she closed the golf course in the late 1920s. Finally, she sold the Hall House and some of the property to Gordon Otto after giving each of the children the remainder. Otto continued the hotel and changed the name to Highlands Manor. All of the children married except Caroline.

MAN OF MYSTERY: PART I

It was a cloudy day and looked like rain. Walking on the side of the road was an old man, apparently well dressed, with a half-full burlap sack slung over his shoulder. I had seen him walking to town on various occasions and decided to give him a ride. After I stopped, he shuffled up to the car and looked in the open window. "Want a ride?" I asked.

"Yes." He answered in a cultured voice.

As he got in, I realized that his well-dressed appearance at a distance was illusionary. His clothes, once well-cut and obviously tailored, were almost in tatters. Even though it was a warm day, he wore a white shirt with a separate collar, tie, vest and jacket. And he smelled. I wasn't sure where he lived, although I had passed him from time to time on the Buck Creek Road.

As if reading my mind, he said, "Just let me off at the Shortoff Road."

I turned off Highway 64 at the Phillips farm onto Buck Creek Road. It was gravel, as were all the secondary roads. I slowed down when I got to Shortoff Road.

"I'll get off here, if you don't mind. I don't want to trouble you any further. Thank you for the ride."

The old man got out and ambled across the bridge over Big Creek as I watched. I was sixteen at the time I gave a ride to the old man, who was known as Colonel "Robinson." Since beginning this series of memories and local history, I have often thought of him. This past winter I started asking several people if they remembered him and if they had any information about who he was. Although a lot of old-timers remembered him, there was very little information they could give me. Several thought he had been well-educated and a well-respected lawyer in the state. Another had heard that he had been ambassador to France and spoke very well. Others remembered him just as a vagrant drunk. I never saw where he lived down Shortoff Road, so I didn't know personally anything more than the chance ride I gave him. So who was Colonel Robinson?

I had heard that at one time he had owned the property where Cold Springs Saddle and Tennis Club is located off Shortoff Road. His name was spelled "Robertson" on the deed rather than "Robinson." Since I started researching Colonel Robinson-Robertson, I found that he was born in North Carolina in 1874. In 1880, he was living in a boardinghouse in Webster with his sister Mary and his mother Laura Woodfin Robertson. She was the daughter of a Macon County physician and was a schoolteacher in Webster. Twenty years later, he was still in Webster and living with his aunt and uncle, Sarah and James Terrell. At that time, he was a lawyer.

On April 2, 1903, he married Laura Amelia Bryson at the then Methodist Episcopal Church South, now the First United Methodist Church, in Franklin. Later on, in September 1918, he registered for the draft. From that registration card, we get a physical glimpse of him. He gave his name as Henry Greene Robertson. He listed his occupation as lawyer. The register listed his height as medium, weight medium, color of eyes hazel, age forty-four and color of hair gray. He listed his next of kin as Mrs. Laura Robertson. I didn't know at the time if this woman was his mother or his wife, though we have recently learned from Mary Ann Sloan that Laura Amelia Bryson, his first wife, later remarried a man from Florida on October 22, 1922. When I found the draft registration document, I gave up trying to find some connection to the army. His title as colonel apparently came from something other than a military rank.

I have talked with several Franklin attorneys, and one gave an explanation for the title of colonel. He said he had heard the title, and at one time was addressed himself as "Colonel," much like some members of the bar place "Esquire" after their name. One piece of the puzzle solved. Another attorney said that he believed Robertson had been a Macon County tax collector, most likely in the 1920s. We find evidence of that in the Macon County Register of Deeds. Another Franklin attorney told me that they have some of Robertson's law books in their law library. The address in the books placed Robertson's office on the second floor of the building where the Frog and Owl Kitchen is located. In 1928, he was one of five trustees, along with Dr. E.R. Gilbert, William Cleaveland, Henry Sloan and W.W. Sullivan, to take title to the Highlands Ball Park.

Robertson did purchase one hundred acres, comprising State Land Grant #961, in 1929 from John Jay Smith and Mary Chapin Smith. Smith had inherited it from his mother, and the grant was originally made to Elias Norton. So there it was. He had bought the property now known as Cold Springs Saddle and Tennis Club. This is off Shortoff Road, and that must have been where he lived when many others and I saw him walking on Buck Creek Road and the Cashiers Road. Now we have him as a resident and property owner in Highlands.

The same day he took title to the Shortoff property, he deeded four acres of it to Marcia G. Viglini of Louisville, Kentucky. Who was Marcia Viglini? And what connection was she to Robertson? The 1930 census shows Marcia Viglini living in Louisville, Kentucky, with her brother Albert. But in 1932, Robertson transferred title of one of two cemetery lots that he had purchased earlier in Woodlawn Cemetery in Franklin to George B. Patton. Marcia V. Robertson, wife, joined him in that sale. So now we have Robertson married a second time.

I have searched all possible records trying to find a record of death for Laura Bryson Robertson, Robertson's first wife, and a marriage record for Marcia Viglini. I did find that Marcia V. Robertson died in Louisville, Kentucky, in 1935, although her place of residence was listed as North Carolina.

Several people have given me insight into the man—those that actually visited his home off Shortoff Road. One described it as a two-story house with terraced gardens and with bushes and trees not native to the area. That person also remembered the interior of the house as being dark and spooky. Another visitor remembers visiting with Robertson. According to his memory, Colonel Robertson had two dogs, Frosty and Andy Gump. He lived mainly on canned food and would toss the empty cans to a corner of the room. He smoked a pipe and didn't bathe. This might be the reason his second wife didn't live with him or left him.

A few years after Marcia died, Robertson sold his one hundred acres to Fred Edwards but retained a life estate. Edwards had a store on Main Street, where Ann Jacob Gallery is now located. One source understood that Robertson was allowed a dollar's worth of groceries a day at Edwards's store. The same source also said that Robertson would visit in Potts Brothers grocery store, where Dutchman's Design is now and was formerly the Highlander Restaurant. He would sit around the old potbellied stove with other old-timers and kibitz.

His health and mostly his mind probably declined to the point where two local physicians, Drs. Ed Angel and William Matthews, found it necessary to find him "mentally disordered." In March 1954, he was committed to Broughton, the state mental hospital in Morganton, North Carolina. Another story was told that a group of prominent North Carolina attorneys raised funds to place Robertson in a private nursing home. Unfortunately, the records at Broughton don't reflect this. He died on his birthday, March 22, 1958, at the age of eighty-four. His remains and those of his mother and aunt can be found in Lot 28, Section A of Woodlawn Cemetery in Franklin. The grave marker is a large, polished granite stone and would have been fairly expensive. It doesn't look almost fifty years old.

In Lot 27, the one he sold back in 1932, lies Judge George B. Patton and his wife. Judge Patton had an illustrious history in Macon County, as well as the state. He was encouraged by unnamed individuals to go to law school after a farming accident caused him to lose a hand. After passing the bar exam before he had completed his first year of law school, he finished the school year and then became a partner in an existing practice in Franklin. This would have been about the same time that Robertson was practicing in Franklin. Patton later ran for the North Carolina legislature and after that became attorney general for the state.

So who was Colonel Henry G. Robinson-Robertson? Records show that his father was a James Robinson. Did his mother change his and her name for some reason? Everyone that knew of him while he was in Highlands called him Colonel Robinson.

When this column came out, one of our good friends and reader of our column, Sarah Talley Crunkleton Davis, called to tell us that her husband knew Colonel Henry Green Robinson/Robertson. After doing a great deal of research on this gentleman for our earlier article, we couldn't wait to interview Charles Davis. Charles was our primary source of information for the piece "Roosevelt's Tree Army" as well.

MAN OF MYSTERY: PART II

As the radio columnist Paul Harvey said many times: "And here is the rest of the story."

To begin with, Charles Davis knew Colonel Robertson personally from the time he milked the colonel's cow back in 1925 until he signed up with the Civilian Conservation Corps in 1935. So let us take you back to 1925, when Charles's family had a home and property near where the first McDonald's drive-in is located just off the bypass in Franklin. Colonel Robertson had a home near the Davis property and lived with his mother and aunt. Charles was slow to point out that the colonel was not very prompt in paying him for the milking.

According to Charles, Laura Robertson, the colonel's mother, was very domineering, so Charles was somewhat of a "momma's boy," even at the age of fifty. She also pronounced his first name as "Henery," adding an extra *e*. She said that a famous author actually spelled his own name with the extra *e*. Laura apparently dominated her sister Sarah Terrell, so it must have been a dysfunctional household.

In 1924, the Peter McCoy building was completed on Main Street in Franklin, and Colonel Robertson had a suite of offices on the second floor, including a large conference room. Also in the 1920s, his mother had a prominent millinery shop in Franklin.

As we told you previously, Laura Bryson was the colonel's first wife. She apparently didn't get along well with the colonel. He was an avid hunter and fisherman and kept good hunting dogs. This, along with the colonel's drinking habits, probably caused Laura to leave him.

The colonel had a large law practice, specializing in real estate and particularly land grants. He was called as an expert witness on land grant matters from the Mississippi River eastward. According to Charles, the colonel had an amazing memory for this sort of information, plus many old maps. It was on one of his trips to the Midwest that he met and married Marcia Viglini. The Viglini family lived in Louisville, Kentucky, and apparently were well-off, as they were large stockholders in Standard Oil. When the colonel purchased the Cold Springs property in 1929, Davis said he understood that Marcia paid for it. The one hundred acres had a nice home and landscaping, and the four acres encompassing the house were transferred into Marcia's name as an individual when the sale was closed.

In 1930, the colonel bought a four-door sedan and hired Charles to be his driver. The trips were mainly to Atlanta, where the colonel conducted real estate business for wealthy Atlantans. They would stay at the Atlanta Athletic Club. It was during this period that Charles became well acquainted with the colonel's drinking habits. He was known to get drunk and sober up as many as three times in one day during these trips. You wonder how a person could do this. Charles said that the colonel had a system whereby he would order a very large meal and then pour syrup over the whole plate. He had an enormous appetite. The colonel explained that the sugar counteracted the alcohol in his system.

It appears that Marcia was also an alcoholic. Since she was living in Louisville, Kentucky, during the 1930 census and died in Louisville in 1935, she and the colonel apparently did not get along.

According to Charles, during the late 1920s the colonel bought and leased land along the Cullasaja River for W.R.C. Smith, an Atlanta business owner. Smith hired local men to patrol the river to prevent people from fishing without Smith's consent.

As an indication of Colonel Robertson's failing mind, in the early 1950s he became lost. Charles Talley went on a search for him. He found the colonel under the cliffs of Shortoff Mountain near his home. One or two of the colonel's dogs were with him. Charles Talley is a brother of Charles Davis's wife Sarah. She figured in our story of the 1940 hurricane that devastated Highlands.

You may have noticed that we have referred to Robertson as the colonel throughout this section, after dispelling it in the first section. According to Charles Davis, the colonel indicated that he had been in France near the Italian border in World War I, either with the Salvation Army or the Red

Cross. He claimed to have acquired the title/rank at that time. This conflicts with his draft registration in Franklin in September 1918. We won't ever know the truth of the matter, though does it really matter?

Henry Green Robertson was apparently a brilliant attorney, sought after by wealthy people all throughout the East. His weakness for liquor dragged him from prominence to pauperdom, and he ultimately lost his mind. We're not here to judge him. At the start, we just wanted to find out about a man whom we had met long ago, and there are still many unanswered questions. But they will have to wait.

We would like to thank all those that helped us with this article: Louis "Bud" Potts, Edward "Buzz" Baty, Charlie McDowell, George Penland, Edna Norton Crisp, Guy Grant of Bryant-Grant Funeral Home, Janet Thomas, Richard Jones, Orville Coward, Pat Patton, Chastity McNeely of Broughton Hospital, Elizabeth Cabe (historian for the First United Methodist Church, Franklin) and Charles Davis.

POCO NO MORE

This is the story of three Bug Hill cottages and one of their owners. Some of the incidents are true and others, well, may just be stories. In 1923, Laura Placidia Bridgers White purchased Lots 3 and 4 from the Highlands Land Company. Placidia White was the wife of Reverend Robb White Jr., an Episcopal priest from Thomasville, Georgia. Her sister, Miss Rebecca Bridgers, bought property nearby in 1924. Placidia found three of the tuberculosis sanatorium cottages (officially known as Highlands Tuberculosis Camp) and had them moved to Lot 3 to form a small house. She named the configuration of cottages Poco No More, or Little No More. The three cottages are now the offices of the Chandler Inn, which is on the west side of Cashiers Road just before the ballpark. Like many people from off the mountain, she had found her cool summer retreat and kept the house for twenty years until she sold it to the duBignon family.

Reverend Robb and Placidia White moved to Thomasville in 1923, the same year she purchased the property in Highlands. Reverend White was born in Lawrenceville, Virginia, in 1878, the son and grandson of Episcopal ministers. Placidia was born near Tarboro, North Carolina, the daughter of John and Laura Bridgers, on January 22, 1881. Her father owned a railroad and farmed. Robb was studying medicine when his father, Reverend Robb

White Sr., rector of Christ Church in Savannah, Georgia, passed away. His last wishes were for Robb to go into the ministry with these words: "Son, if you want to help people, why not help the most important part of them… their souls?" So Robb Jr. dropped medicine and went into the ministry.

About 1908, after graduation from seminary and marriage, the Whites became Protestant missionaries and moved from Placidia's parents' home, where their first child Laura was born, to the Philippines, at a place called Bontoc. An Episcopal church and mission school was founded in 1906, and that is where the Whites lived and taught. The school's name is All Saints Mission Elementary School, is still in existence today and has its own website. It was in a village amongst the Igarot tribe in North Luzon. This was at the time of the Philippine Insurrection, and there was fighting going on throughout the Philippines between the U.S. Army and the various Philippine tribes. While the Whites were living there, Territorial Governor-General William C. Forbes befriended them. Forbes left the Philippines the same year as the Whites. He was later appointed as ambassador to Japan in the early '30s. Although from Massachusetts, he later followed the White family to Thomasville, where he spent the winters and raised horses.

A ship's passenger list from Manila to San Francisco shows that Placidia returned to the United States in 1913 from the Philippines with sons Robb III, who was born in 1909 in the Philippines, and John. The next time we catch up with Robb White Jr., he had joined the U.S. Army as a chaplain, and he served in France in World War I. The 1920 census records indicate that the family—including Placidia, Robb III, Laura, John and Rebecca "Beck" but not Reverend Robb Jr.—was living with Placidia's parents near Tarboro, North Carolina. In 1923 the family moved to Thomasville, Georgia, where Reverend White had taken the call to be rector of St. Thomas Episcopal Church.

According to Robert C. Balfour's *History of St. Thomas Church*, Reverend White arrived in Thomasville, Georgia, with his family, still wearing his army uniform. Much of what we know about his tenure at St. Thomas is based on Robert Balfour's book and Robb White III's article in the July 1953 issue of *Reader's Digest*, "The Most Unforgettable Character I've Met." He became known as Preacher White to everyone in and around Thomasville. He had taken his father's advice to heart long before he reached Thomasville. As Robert C. Balfour writes in his *History of St. Thomas Church*, "He became a one-man welfare department. He solicited funds from many of the townspeople as well as the 'winter residents' to provide money for food,

Robb White Jr. in Tarboro, North Carolina at Placidia's parents' home. *Courtesy of Robb White IV.*

clothes, housing, nurses, and even helpers to carry on the work he loved and stressed more than life itself."

Preacher White's caring for people's souls went beyond the usual discretionary funds normally provided by the church. Balfour continues:

> *On many occasions he filled the hospital with indigent patients and much to the credit of the hospital and the doctors, not the first person was refused admittance. Through this hospital connection, Dr. Charles Wall and Preacher White became warm friends. Dr. Wall joined the Episcopal Church and became a great churchman.*
>
> *Anyone in need or distress contacted Preacher White for help. The railroad police picked up a young boy beating a ride on a freight train going*

Placidia White in Tarboro, North Carolina at Placidia's parents' home. *Courtesy of Robb White IV.*

to Florida. Preacher White learned about the arrest, bailed the boy out, took him to the church rectory, gave him a bath, and a good night's sleep, bought him a ticket to St. Petersburg, Florida and wished him well as he sent him on his way." That boy turned out very well. We all know him as "Pepper" Martin formerly of the St. Louis Cardinals.

On another occasion, Balfour relates, "One cold, damp winter night I went to choir practice and wore my overcoat. When the practice was over I couldn't find my coat. Preacher White soon set me straight by explaining that a cold, miserably wet stranger came by the church and he gave him my coat. As an afterthought he added, 'I had already given mine away.'"

Here is an excerpt from Robb White III's article in *Reader's Digest*:

He never learned to drive a car. He tried but there was none of the communion between my father and the engine that there was between him and a horse. When distances became too great for horses…He began hitchhiking…When he wanted to go somewhere he walked into the middle of traffic and stood there.

…I can see him now. A gaunt man, face even more hawklike in middle age. An unbelievably unkempt man (but always clean; he washed his own shirts and underwear and never ironed them) with his tie adrift under one ear and in clothes which never seemed to fit. Most of the time they didn't, for he invariably gave away anything he had and dressed in what he could borrow.

…My father never knew it but his own family stood deep in the ranks of the poor. [His mother Placidia] *made ends meet by teaching horseback riding* [she trained Forbes's horses], *she farmed, sculpted, and painted pictures to sell.*

There are so many stories about this country preacher. We wish we could relate all of them. He was only sick twice, according to Robb III. Once he had appendicitis and almost died before he got to the hospital because he was detoured trying to get milk to children, who had no milk, by walking a cow four miles to their house. The only other time was when the doctor diagnosed him with ALS, Lou Gehrig's disease. The doctor told him that "he would lose control of his muscles, would feel no pain and remain mentally alert, possibly for five years." Dad said, "Useless?" After that his father asked Placidia and Robb III to remember him, closed his eyes and died.

His actions may well be described as saintly, but one parishioner may have said it best. "Years after his death—if our name, Robb White, is mentioned, there will be a pause, a look, and someone will say, 'People sure loved the Preacher.'"

As we have said, Preacher White and Placidia had four children: Laura, Robb III, John and Rebecca. Robb IV has provided us information about those children, his aunts and uncle, as well as his father. Laura was called "Pats" and married a succession of wealthy men. John, perhaps the most unusual of the four, was a lifetime researcher for the Smithsonian Museum and co-authored the book *Stonehenge Decoded*. Some of his eccentricities include living in the same room he rented while attending Harvard and driving the same car for his whole life. He was the world's authority on unicorns and was said to have been the first man to run the Boston Marathon naked. Rebecca, called "Beck," like Laura was a great beauty. She was a skilled but unknown artist and sculptor in addition to being a horse trainer, like her mother Placidia, and a documentary filmmaker.

Robb III had an interesting career. He graduated from the United States Naval Academy in 1931 and served in World War II rising from ensign to captain. His other jobs were with E.I. DuPont, as a construction engineer, deckhand on a ship to the West Indies and finally author. He wrote over twenty books, including *Deathwatch, Surrender, House on Haunted Hill, Up Periscope* and *Silent Ship*. He was a prolific contributor to the *Saturday Evening Post, True, Esquire, Atlantic* and the *Naval Institute*. From the Robb White papers, McCain Library Archives, he is quoted as saying that young people liked his works the most. He attributed this to their good, decent and courageous nature—exactly the sort of people about whom he enjoyed writing.

Robb White III and his wife, Rosalie Mason, had three children: Robb IV, Barbara and June. Robb IV and June still live in Thomasville, Georgia, and both are published authors. June has written under the name of June B. White and Bailey White. Her books include *Mama Makes up her Mind and Other Dangers of Southern Living, Quite a Year for Plums, Sleeping at the Starlight Motel* and *Buttercups and Bittersweet*. She is also a frequent contributor to the PBS radio show *All Things Considered* with comments on daily life in a small southern town. She has been teaching first grade in Thomasville for over twenty years.

Robb White IV is author of *How to Build a Tin Canoe* and boat stories for magazines, including *Messing About in Boats*, a publication that covers boats and stories from the Republic of Georgia to the South China Sea. Robb has been in the boat-building business for some forty years, with sons and grandchildren who have apprenticed in his business. He now has a busy public speaking schedule including boat shows and, most recently, speaking at the Sewanee University Library.

Isabel and I corresponded with Robb III at the time we owned the property Poco No More (the Burlap Bag) when he was handling his Aunt Rebecca Bridgers's estate. He told us several anecdotes about his parents that we have retold many times. One incident was about a man in Highlands who had been harassing Placidia. One day he followed her up the stairs to her sister Rebecca's house. She apparently had enough of his actions and shot him. We're not sure whether she killed the man or wounded him, and we've never been able to find anyone who could confirm this story. Another anecdote concerned his father. Preacher White would invite people in Thomasville to visit their home in Highlands. The people would show up unannounced, and Placidia grew tired of her unexpected guests.

It wasn't until now, when we read Robert Balfour's *History of St. Thomas Church* and Robb III's *Reader's Digest* article, that we can understand what kind of man Preacher White was. His invitations to his friends were only in keeping with his sharing of whatever he had with others. Preacher White died on November 12, 1946, and Placidia died on February 25, 1955.

Reverend Robb White Jr. was a truly remarkable man. He could speak six languages and read a dozen more. And just as remarkable are the generations that followed him and Placidia: authors, artists, researchers, documentary film producers, horse trainers and radio personalities.

In the records of visiting ministers at our Church of the Incarnation, Reverend Robb White Jr. held services here in the late summer of 1928. We don't know how often he came to Highlands, but that summer he was our priest. (He must have returned to Thomasville by the end of August or early September since Isabel's parents, Tudor and Margaret Hall, were married at Incarnation September 19, 1928, by the Presbyterian minister because Incarnation was closed for the winter (although the ceremony took place in our church.) Her sister, Rebecca Bridgers, gave the Processional Cross at the Church of the Incarnation in memory of Laura Placidia White.

Over the years since Placidia sold the property, there have been five owners: Charles and Barton Terrell duBignon, Curt and Mildred Wilson, Tudor Hall Associates (Tudor and Margaret Hall's real estate and insurance company), ourselves (Tony and Isabel) and Randolph Power. The duBignons used the house for their summer home, selling it in 1947 to the Wilsons. Curt and Mildred raised their family there, as well as built a warehouse for their plumbing and electrical business. When they sold the property to Tudor Hall Associates, the warehouse was used for the company's building division, Village Service, and an employee, Morris Wilson, and his family used the house. When Isabel and I bought the property, Isabel opened the Burlap Bag, a boutique selling gifts and women's clothes. I opened up a real estate and insurance office in the front room of the old warehouse, and gradually we renovated the rest of the warehouse into shops. This was our son Tom Chambers's first job as an independent contractor. Later we added a two-story wing to the warehouse. At one time or another there was a Brass Rubbing Studio, the first Christmas shop in Highlands, a hairdresser, a music store, a jeweler, an antique shop, a Far East gift shop, an art supply store and art gallery, a manicurist and a Thai restaurant. When we sold the property to Randy Power, he converted it into a bed-and-breakfast, the Chandler Inn.

With four generations of Robb Whites in our story, we have identified Robb White the Naval Academy graduate and author as Robb III, and Robb White the author and boat builder as Robb IV for clarification purposes only. We would also like to thank Reverend Charles Bennett, present rector of St. Thomas Church, Thomasville, and Robb White IV for their help and contributions to our research.

After the second of the two articles had been published, we were told by a friend from Macon, Georgia, that Johns Hopkins University would send their first-year medical students to the hospital in Thomasville. About the same time, we learned that Robb White IV had died. We had just mailed him copies of the first and second articles, the April and May 2006 issues of Laurel *magazine. It was a sad ending to a remarkable family history and one who helped us write it.*

MISS HANCKEL AND MISS NOURSE

Two women were walking down the Piazzle Degli Uffizi in the hot August sun. A humid breeze was blowing off the River Arno one block away. The older of the two was carrying a small collapsible easel, and the younger, possibly a daughter, carried two artist's paint boxes and a large pad of drawing paper. They were speaking in Italian about Germany's invasion of Belgium and France. They thought they should make plans to move to Rome since they had recently vacated the villa of a friend who had returned to Florence and were staying in a small apartment near the gallery. It was 1914 and Europe was beginning to feel the effects of the start of World War I. As they approached their destination, the Uffizi Gallery, they stopped talking out of respect for the visitors and other art students studying there.

It's not often that we get to tell you about two talented and interesting women, whom Isabel knew as a child. They built one of the early houses on Big Bear Pen, and we decided to do some research about them, as no one had before, or so we thought. Miss Nourse was born in 1858 in Whitby, England, and later emigrated from there to Canada. The only other record we have is the 1880 census, during which time she was living in Rochester, New York, with her American-born mother. Miss Hanckel was born on May 16, 1875, in Charleston, South Carolina, to Anne Matilda Heyward and Charles P. Hanckel. Miss Hanckel had two brothers and six sisters. Only one brother married, and one sister died before reaching adulthood.

We don't know where Miss Hanckel and Miss Nourse met, but we believe it was sometime after 1901. In 1910, the federal census shows them living in Manhattan, New York. We recently discovered that they had been attending

The Hanckel-Nourse home.

Columbia University, studying art, although a request from Barnard College drew a blank. The only other college at Columbia that admitted women at that time was Teachers College. They were known to have traveled in Europe and lived in Italy. In August 1914, Miss Hanckel wrote to her mother, then living in Flat Rock, North Carolina. This was just after war had broken out and the German army was marching on Paris. The letter indicated that they had been studying at the Uffizi Gallery in Florence and were concerned about booking passage back to the United States. Italy was originally on the side of Germany at the start of the war but changed to the side of the other European countries when Austria invaded northern Italy.

They apparently returned to the United States shortly after leaving Florence and settled near Miss Hanckel's mother. The 1920 census lists them in Hendersonville, North Carolina. They may have gone back to Europe later. In 1926, they bought two lots from S.P. Ravenel Jr. and Albertina Staub in the Big Bear Pen Home Development Company subdivision. Since we couldn't locate them in the 1930 census, it's possible they again returned to Italy. In June 1935, they returned to the United States from Naples.

After all their travels, they bought several more lots on the top of Big Bear Pen Mountain and built their house in 1936. Isabel thought that Roy Phillips may have built their house, and Ran Shaffner confirmed it. Edna Phillips

Bryson had loaned the Highlands Historical Society her father's scrapbook with photographs of the houses that he had built. The Hanckel-Nourse House was on one page of the scrapbook with the heading "1936."

The house was built, as some have said, in the Italianate style, possibly inspired by villas where the two lived in Italy. It was definitely not the typical mountain architecture of the time. It sits next to one of the reserved lots with a view of Whiteside Mountain and Highlands Falls. Although it has been bought and sold many times since the two friends died in 1951, it still remains basically the same structure on the outside. It was one of the first houses built after E.I. Davis, several others from Greenwood, South Carolina, and Frank B. Cook of Highlands started the development.

We have talked to several people who recall their names but few who remember anything about them. We don't believe they were reclusive; it's just that most of those who worked for them or visited them are gone. Doris Potts recalls that Aunt Nellie Zoellner looked after Miss Hanckel when she developed Parkinson's disease. Buzz Baty remembers that Frank Carpenter from Scaly Mountain was their last caretaker and possibly their driver. They had a two-car garage built next to the house, but perhaps neither of them drove. There was a servant's apartment underneath the garage.

Isabel's recollections seem to be the best way to bring these two women to life:

I remember going with my father, Tudor Hall, to the house when they needed changes to the electrical system. At that time, I would wait in the truck while he made the changes. He was the electrical contractor when the house was built. Later on, I got to go into the house when my mother, Margaret, took art lessons from Miss Nourse. When you went in the side door there was a big entrance hall with wide stairs that went up to the living room on the second floor. The stair risers were lower than normal as the two women were both short. The living room was large with a bank of windows facing the view of Highlands Falls. On the right side of the room was a masonry fireplace faced in Italian tile. There were comfortable sofas on either side of the fireplace with lots of pillows. Books were everywhere in the room and in the library adjoining the living room. Near the front windows were two painting easels. I usually sat in one of the chairs watching mother paint. Sometimes Miss Nourse was hooking a rug and mother watched and learned how to do that. On the view side of the living room between the windows, there was a single French door that opened into the air. There wasn't any deck or porch at that time. The ladies told us that that was a spirit door. I wondered at the time what "spirits" were.

Sometimes Miss Hanckel sat at small table working with an awl making rather crude leather sandals. She said they were very comfortable. Today they would be similar to Birkenstocks. She said she learned how to make them when they lived in Italy. In the winter, she wore socks with her sandals. I can remember seeing them walk to town when they passed our house on Fifth Street. Once, when we came for mother's art lesson, I saw Miss Nourse sitting up in a tree. She loved to climb and said she would do it until she died. So when you look at the large trees near their house, you might see Miss Nourse still there. I was impressed by both of the women's creativity, and at Miss Nourse's active life.

We know from various genealogical sources, and one distant cousin, that Miss Hanckel was an Episcopalian. In the late 1940s or possibly 1950, Miss Nourse fell and broke her hip and was hospitalized in Franklin. She subsequently developed pneumonia and died in February 1951 at age ninety-two. My parents attended a memorial service at their house. Dr. A. Rufus Morgan, our rector at the time, officiated at the service outside. According to Miss Nourse's request in her will, her remains were to be cremated and the ashes cast out on the mountain. Unfortunately, there was an updraft that blew the ashes back onto those gathered and into the trees beside the house, where Miss Nourse loved to climb. There is a small stone niche in the amphitheatre-like area at the front of the house. It is said that the remainder of Miss Nourse's ashes are buried there.

Miss Hanckel's battle with Parkinson's was long fought, but she finally went to a nursing home in Columbia, South Carolina. She died in November 1951 at age seventy-five and was buried in Magnolia Cemetery in Charleston, South Carolina, along with her family. Two of her sisters, Marion Stuart Hanckel and Sarah Hanckel, who never married, lived with their mother, Anne, until she died.

Miss Nourse and Miss Hanckel deeded the property to and from each other in 1926, as tenants-in-common with right of survivorship. Miss Nourse's will left everything to Miss Hanckel. Miss Hanckel's will provided money and jewelry to one of her sisters, various cousins and one of their employees. The house was left to Dr. Richard W. Hanckel, a distant cousin from Charleston, South Carolina. We spoke with his son recently, and he remembers coming up to the house on summer vacations with his family. The house was sold in 1959 and passed through various hands. Isabel's father sold the house to Virgil and Elizabeth (Betty) Griffin, from Chicago, in 1972. Virgil had a publishing company in Chicago, and Betty had been a student at the Art Institute in Chicago. They had traveled all over the world, and the house was perfectly suited to their taste and collection of art. Betty was at the forefront, early on, to establish a performing arts center. Her dream was realized years after her death with the establishment of the Martin-Lipscomb Performing Arts Center on Chestnut Street. A year after Virgil died in 1974, my father helped her sell the house to Richard and Gay Kattel. At that time, Richard Kattel was president of Citizens and Southern National Bank and lived in Atlanta. Many of you probably remember when he and Gay would fly up to Highlands in the C&S helicopter and land at the ballpark. The Kattels owned the house for twenty-five years, made several changes to the interior and added a deck off the living room.

The current owners, Jerry and Mary Catherine Temple, invited us to look at the house and share what they had gathered and accumulated about the house, as well as information about Miss Hanckel and Miss Nourse. Cathy gave us a tour from top to basement. Isabel and Cathy Temple compared notes on what Isabel remembered. We want to say that a few additions have been made, and the porch off the kitchen has been enclosed, but the restoration has kept the house true to its original owners. We believe that they would have approved the changes. The Temples have kept all the original hardware, the restoration of the hardwood floors and the return of inset window benches. They have retained the original windows and added storm windows on the outside. During the tour, Cathy showed us dress hangers with a wooden handle that had been adapted by the women. This allowed them to hang their long dresses on the high clothes rods of their closets; otherwise they couldn't have cleared the floor. Other notes from Gay Kattel's history of the women and the house include reference to the library of well over one hundred books in German, Italian and Japanese, as well as many books in English. There were Morse code symbols in several of the books. The subject matter ran the gamut from poetry and philosophy to politics. Possibly Miss Hanckel studied architecture, as there were handwritten drawings of the building requirements, which were professionally described. There was a dumbwaiter from the basement to the second floor and electric buzzers in each bedroom connected to the kitchen. We have not been able to establish the direct connection with Dr. Richard W. Hanckel, who inherited the house, and Miss Mary Bull Hanckel. Miss Hanckel's father Charles may have been a brother to Christian Hanckel, who was Dr. Richard W. Hanckel's grandfather.

We want to thank Richard W. Hanckel, son of Dr. Richard W. Hanckel, Doris Potts, Buzz Baty, Edna Phillips Bryson, Dr. Ran Shaffner and especially Jerry and Cathy Temple for the information and material that they have provided. We recently discovered that a great-great-great-uncle Reverend Dr. J.S. Hanckel was a supply clergy from Charleston at Calvary Episcopal Church in Fletcher, North Carolina, in the 1860s.

THE RAGLAND CABIN

Last December, the Highlands Historical Society held its annual Christmas Show house at the old Joe Webb log cabin on Bear Pen Mountain. It's not often that Isabel and I have a repeated connection with one of Highlands' older historic homes. The Ragland cabin is one of the oldest homes on Bear Pen Mountain and is the subject of one of the more interesting summer resident families. So let us begin with how the cabin came to be.

The log home was built by Joe Webb and his stepson Furman Vinson for Nathaniel Thomas Ragland and Maude Buchanan Ragland about 1927–28. The Raglands purchased the two lots on Bear Pen, as well as acreage in the Mirror Lake area in 1925. The logs for the cabin came from the Mirror Lake property. It was to be a summer residence for the Ragland family who lived in Miami, Florida, where they owned a chain of movie theatres. Although the cabin has had many owners since then, and various owners have added to the furniture and structure, there are a number of pieces of furniture that Mr. Ragland himself made for the cabin. Some of the pieces include the birch cabinet in the corner of the living room near the porch, the round dining table with a lazy Susan, a desk in the bedroom off the back porch and the porch swing, to name a few. Birch was not commonly used for furniture in Highlands, but similar birch trees can be found on the property near the site where the chimney stones were quarried. The old springhouse near the cabin is still there. The grandchildren remember going to it where milk, watermelons and other foods were kept cool.

The Raglands grew up in Jeffersontown, Kentucky, outside of Louisville, and had two sons: Howard Carleton, born on February 19, 1902, and Thomas Rucker, born in 1904. Shortly after Rucker was born, Mr. Ragland

Ragland Cabin on Big Bear Pen.

contracted typhoid fever, which damaged his lungs. His doctors advised him to move west. The young family moved to Oklahoma in 1905 with friend John Rucker and then to New Mexico the next year. The area had no name, and the Raglands opened a blacksmith shop, general store and post office. When the Postal Service contacted Maude, who became the first postmistress in New Mexico, about the name of the town, Mr. Ragland was quoted as saying, "Ragland, I guess." The town is still there and is near Tucumcari. Shortly before they left New Mexico (and possibly their reason for leaving), there occurred an old Wild West–style flare-up between the Mexicans and a number of cowboys. For some reason, Maude Ragland hid all the knives in the store, probably for fear of becoming involved.

The family moved back to Kentucky in 1909, then to Jacksonville, Florida, in 1910 and then on to Punta Gorda, Florida, where Mr. Ragland bought the Seminole Hotel. During that time, former president Teddy Roosevelt and the current governor of Florida, Albert Gilchrist, stayed at the Seminole. In 1915, the Raglands returned to Kentucky, where Mr. Ragland contracted pleurisy and pneumonia, possibly brought on by the damage to his lungs from the typhoid fever he contracted in Kentucky. Some say he was fortunate, as he stumbled and fell one day, breaking one of his ribs and punctured one lung. The deflation of that lung actually cured his pleurisy.

The next year they moved to Sarasota, Florida, and opened a movie theatre. He registered for the draft in1917 at age forty-one but did not serve. The family made their last move and settled in Miami, where Mr. Ragland owned and operated the Peninsular Real Estate Company and a chain of movie theatres in Miami; Hialeah, Florida; and Nassau, British West Indies. One of the stories told about Mr. Ragland includes a real estate investment deal offered by a man from Chicago. It turned out that the deal being proposed came from Al Capone. Mr. Ragland turned it down.

Later on, Paramount Pictures tried to force Mr. Ragland into selling his theatres by threatening to open their theatres near the Ragland establishments. Mr. Ragland refused to sell, and soon after that, Paramount and other major Hollywood movie companies were taken to court on federal antitrust charges. Mr. Ragland later sold his theatres to Wometco, a national theatre chain.

On December 1, 1929, Rucker Ragland married Catherine Eloise Rice at the Episcopal church in Highlands. Tom Harbison, son of Professor Thomas G. Harbison, served as best man. The church was cold, as there was only a small coal stove for heat, and Tom fainted. They tried to carry him into the sacristy, where he could be laid out. Trouble was, Tom was taller than the sacristy was long. He was dating Elizabeth Rice at the time, and she was Eloise's sister. Isabel's parents were in attendance, as Eloise was Margaret's best friend. So the Rice, Lowe and Harbison families are all cousins to the Raglands.

Another story about Mr. Ragland concerns the Sears, Roebuck store in Miami. This could have been during the Depression. The store manager contacted Mr. Ragland when their cash flow got so low that he couldn't make the payroll one week. Apparently, Mr. Ragland was known for his wealth, as well as his philanthropy. Mr. Ragland loaned the store enough to make the payroll.

Isabel recently talked to Pricilla Ragland Russ, Ruck and Eloise's daughter, and compared notes with her about the Ragland home in Miami. Eloise and Ruck were living there at the time that the Hall family was invited down to Miami during the winter of 1937. The house was on Okeechobee Road, across from a canal. Isabel remembers that the house was tremendous—five bedrooms and five baths, according to Prissy. Isabel asked her about her grandparents' bedroom, which was very large with wood floors and took up the entire second floor. Isabel remembered that the Raglands had told her parents that it had been owned by some famous person. Coming from Highlands and hardly ever out of the state, it seemed like a mansion to Isabel. Prissy said the house had been built by a famous band leader of the time. She thinks that the bedroom could have been used by the band itself. Mr. Ragland was quite a joker, according to Prissy. Isabel found that out when he explained to her one morning at breakfast that he went out to the canal early every morning to milk the sea cows. Isabel had a sensitive stomach and avoided milk from then on.

Prissy remembers coming to Highlands every summer along with her brother Roger and cousin Nat. They all grew up in the cabin. Later, after the cabin was sold, they would come visit their other grandparent, Luther Rice.

Prissy likened her father to the Indian athlete Jim Thorpe. He was very athletic. At one time, he was watching the boxer Gene Tunney work out with sparing partners. When Tunney worked through several, he asked if anyone wanted to go a round with him. Ruck volunteered and was promptly knocked down by Tunney. Then he got up and knocked Tunney down. That ended the match as far as Tunney was concerned. Another time, he was swimming out to a barge and met Johnny Weissmuller. He and Weissmuller swam together that day.

In the movie industry, Ruck was known as "Smokey" Ragland. His job was key grip and construction coordinator. His credits include *They Were Expendable*, *PT 109*, *Flipper* and many others filmed in Florida. He met and became friends with many well-known actors. Prissy became involved in the entertainment industry when she and her husband Terry worked for Walt Disney. Both were artists and sculptors. Terry worked on building Epcot. Roger worked in many positions, like his father, in the production side of films, as well as appearing as an actor in *North and South*, *The Blue and the Gray* and other films. Nathaniel "Nat" Thomas Ragland started in the movie industry like his cousins but switched to running his own charter boat.

As we mentioned in the beginning, both Isabel and I and now our son, Tom Chambers, have had many connections with both the family and the cabin. Isabel remembers visiting with the Raglands as a child, here and in Florida. Many years later, when Isabel's brother, Tudor G. "Buddy" Hall, married Suzanne Koepp-Baker in Highlands in 1956, the then owners of the cabin, Frank and Helene Talbot, offered use of the cabin to us and our children, as well as Isabel's sister Sarah, her husband Russell Paxton and their children. At a recent Thanksgiving, Sarah and Russell's granddaughter, Lisa, came to Highlands to be married, and history repeated itself. The new owners of the cabin are Tom and Vickie Chambers, and they offered the cabin to Tom's cousin, Sally Paxton Wilcox, and her family, parents of the bride Lisa Wilcox, as well as Russell Paxton and his second wife, Vickie. And it all began from Margaret Hall being best friend to Eloise Rice.

After the cabin was sold in the early '50s, it was owned by a number of families. We have already mentioned the Talbot family, who enjoyed it for ten years after the Raglands sold it. Virginia Talbot, one of the Talbots' daughters, returned to Highlands to live year round and enjoys her involvement with the Highlands Community Players. The Goldsmith family from Atlanta owned the cabin from the early 1970s to 2003. Turner Goldsmith was an officer of the John Harland Company in Atlanta. His daughter, Kathy, inherited the cabin and sold it to Tom Chambers, who was a friend of Kathy's brother. As an antique log cabin builder and restorer, he has restored a number of Joe Webb cabins and looks forward to doing the same to the Ragland Cabin.

We want to thank Harold C. Ragland's son, Nathaniel "Nat" Thomas Ragland, and Thomas Rucker Ragland's son and daughter, Roger and Prissy Maude Ragland Russ, who provided most of the information for this brief history. Jessie Harbison Sheldon also helped get this started, with Isabel filling in many details.

PART III

History and Other Interesting Vignettes of Highlands

This section covers a lot ground in years, from the Civil War to the early 1950s. If you sense a little of *Cold Mountain* in "Letters from a Soldier," you'd be right. And after you read "Who Maintained Our Roads Back When?" you'll appreciate the North Carolina Department of Transportation a little more. Perhaps not for what the DOT does but rather that you as a resident don't have to look after the roads yourself.

LETTERS FROM A SOLDIER

Many of you have seen the PBS special created by Ken Burns on the Civil War. Much of the narrative in the special was taken from letters written home by soldiers in both the North and South. A new book was published last year that is also composed of letters from soldiers in various wars.

We would like to bring you closer to home with a few letters from one of our own, David Norton, my great-grandfather, son of Roderick and grandson of early pioneer Barak Norton.

David "Dave" Norton was twenty-seven years old when he enlisted in the Confederate army as a private in Company B, known as the Jackson Guards, on July 17, 1862. He was promoted to third lieutenant on December 29, 1862. This company became part of the Army of Northern Virginia under General Robert E. Lee. These letters were written to his first wife, Mary Holden Norton, who died in 1868.

Camp near Weldon, NC
Aug. 23, 1863

My own Dear wife,

With the greatest of pleasure I again drop you a short note. Mary it has been such a short time since I have wrote you that I can not have much news to write. My health is improving, I am about well but I feel some what on the dull order today from the fact that I was on guard dewty last night my bed was the ground and my pillow a small black gum log. Though I rested fine I feel very much like I was at home since I got back to camp.

You ast me to write you if Gen. Ransom arrested me or punished me in truth he has not yet. I don't suppose he will. There has but 3 other officers of the Regt come in as of yet and had I got my orders I would have been home this good Sabbath day. I had orders to remain at home until the 24th inst. I wish I had got my orders. I will send you some money by Mr. Hooper. I will inform you of the amt. Before I close, I will say no more this evening. Monday 24. Inst. Monday morning has come we have been out on drill now I will say a few more words. Had I got my orders I would been at home this morning with you in place of being in camp.

I hope this will find you all in good health. And doing well. Mary I will now go on to state to you what the camps put me in mind of. More like a camp meeting than any army of men. We have two sermons every day if not more. I have heard one good sermon this good Sabbath morning and expect to hear another this evening…we have a Presbyterian preacher and 14 has joined the church or professed religion and some 50 mourners seeking religion. We have a big revival in the Regt. I hope they will hold out faithful and reform for it is badly needed in our Regt.

I heard this morning that Fort Sumpter was all tore to peaces, but I do not know true it is we hear so much that is false. I hope it is not true. There is no talk of any fighting around this place. At present though the Yanks may make one of their raids soon. We have some warm weather here at this time. I think I sweat at least one quart a day. The air are not like it is in Hamburg. I would much rather be in good old Hamburg. Sitting facing the gentle zephyrs. But I am very well satisfied. Camp life suits me better than to be out in the mountains. I will say no more today. I will write you some tomorrow continue my letter–

Dave had been wounded in battle and just returned from sick furlough when he wrote this next letter. He had been nursed by a woman named Meta before going home. Mary gave birth to a daughter in April 1864, and Dave named her Meta after the nurse.

Petersburg, Va
August 25th 1864

My own wife,

I again take pleasure to write you in answer yours (of 18th), which gave me much pleasure to hear from you and hear that you was well. I have not had a letter from you til today for 3 weeks. I am tolerable well. I hope you are all well…You need not entreat me to come so much for it is my full intention to come first opportunity. Sure enough Bill & Dick have gone to the yanks. Pitty but they could have gone up in front of Petersburg on 30th July, we could have sent them to their loving home…

I am sorrow to tell you that [name indecipherable] *died yesterday 24th this Inst. of his wound I did not think he would die though he was mortally wounded. Nothing strang has occurred since I last wrote you mortar shelling and sharp shooting is just as common to us as the dogs barking and the chickens cackling is to you all, we do not pay any attention to it, though we loose men daily.*

I must tell you that our ditches are very filthy since it has rained so much these trenches are filthy than any hog lot you ever saw in your life and smell worse sour the sink. I never you know yourself have been in favor of this cruel war and the longer the worse…I would love to see you and the children. Give my respects to your mother and family. Excuse bad writing, your loving husband. Dave

David was in Petersburg, Virginia, for at least five months. This was also the sight of the famous Battle of the Crater. Across from him in the Union lines was John Durgin.

The Ditches
Sept 13 1864

My Dear Wife,

I send you $54.00 Dollars by R. V. Hix all five dollar bills except two of them are two dollar notes. I will direct him to leave them at the Penlands…I have got no more time to write you anything. Hix starts in a minute.

Your loving husband, Dave

P.S. I got a slight wound yesterday the skin just graise on both shoulders none to do any hurt. I did not go out of the trenches it was done by the explosion of a mortar shell.

This next letter sounds the most cheerful of the many that Dave wrote.

In the same old Ditches near Petersburg, Va
Decr. 2ⁿᵈ 1864

My own Dear Wife,

With great pleasure I will again drop you a note after eating a hearty dinner. I am in the best of health and getting as fat as an old stag. I hope this will find you all in good health. I have not heard from you for two weeks. I wish I could get a letter from you. I begin to want to hear the news if you have any. I must brag to you a little about how well I have been living since I have got my box. I cooked a big dinner day before yesterday and invited Col. Rutledge, Maj. Love, Capts. Freeman and Moxing up to take dinner with me. They accordingly did so; we taken a few drinks of brandy we then proceeded to take our dinner which was the best dinner that had been eat in these ditches…in the mean time Gen. Ransom came along the lines I presented to him of the finest apples you sent me. He thanked me very much.

…I am a thousand times oblige to you for the box and hope I will be able to pay you for the same in the future…J.P. Slatton was one (who was killed) he reced a slight wound in the arm done by a peace of a shell. I did not see him though they told me it was of a dangerous wound I was very sorrow, he was my [?] only mate. He done our cooking though I can cook as good as any Lady in the Confederate States…Mary I mean to send upon application for a furlough this evening though I doubt about getting. So you need not look for me for I have no idea of getting it. Look for me when

you see me coming and not before. Kiss the little children for me. I am your husband. Dave

Dave Norton did get his furlough, directly from General Robert E. Lee, survived the war and returned to Whiteside Cove. Mary died in 1868, and Dave married Martha Adams. The family moved to Highlands in 1888 and purchased the Central House hotel. In 1895, Dave, his future son-in-law Tudor Tucker Hall, Dr. Henry T. O'Farrell, Jeremiah Pierson and Meta Norton Frost, Dave's daughter and widow of Dr. Charles Frost, were founding members of the Episcopal church in Highlands. The Nortons later moved out of town to what is now the Main Street Inn. Dave served for four years as postmaster. His great-granddaughter is Isabel, your co-author.

Dave died in 1912 and is buried in Highlands Memorial Park.

Another great-granddaughter, Joanna Hall Moylan, transcribed Dave's handwritten letters onto the typewriter several years ago. We have included some of these letters.

ROOSEVELT'S TREE ARMY

Your authors were not aware of this organization, but we do remember the Civilian Conservation Corps, which was created in 1933 to put literally hundreds of thousands of young men between the ages of seventeen and twenty-five to work. Over the life of the Corps, approximately 2.5 million men served from 1933 to 1942.

We remember a number of projects attributed to the CCC, but we wanted to talk to someone who knew firsthand about the "tree army." Charles H. Davis now lives in Otto with his wife, Sarah Talley Crunkleton Davis. Charles remembers well as he was assigned to the camp located in Horse Cove. We sat down with Charles and Sarah last week and heard his story. He had worked earlier on the graveling of the Franklin Road in the early '30s as a jackhammer man and in the process picked up the nickname of "Jack."

The first camp in Macon County was located off U.S. 441 behind where the Whistle Stop Mall is now. About two hundred men were brought up from Georgia and set down in a blackberry patch with tents and a field kitchen. The next morning over 10 percent had "gone over the hill." Charles wanted to sign up and asked Henry Baty for help. Henry was in charge of the ranger district at that time. Charles didn't qualify under the existing

Charles Davis.

criteria. His family had to be on relief. This was in 1935, and he was twenty-two years old. Henry got him qualified as a LEM (local experienced man). Camp F-19 was moved from Dahlonega, Georgia, to Horse Cove with two hundred young men. That was the usual size of a camp. A regular army officer supervised each camp. In this case, it was a Captain F.C. Chandler.

The camps were run as if they were an army unit, with drills, mess halls and more. The only difference was that they didn't have to do the Manual of Arms, which is a drill performed by the army in the use of and handling of rifles in formation. The pay was thirty dollars per month, with twenty-five dollars being sent to the men's homes. The camps in north Georgia and Western North Carolina were supplied by the army at Fort McPherson in Atlanta.

Charles said that he couldn't really live on five dollars a month so he bought a 1928 Buick. Being somewhat of a ladies' man, he would take off to Highlands in the evening and do some courting. He also purchased whiskey to resell to his friends in camp. This augmented his income.

One of the first jobs that this camp did was to build or improve the road from Horse Cove down through Bull Pen to NC 107. Charles became the truck driver in a Model T truck at this time and hauled gravel. Later, he was asked to help carry supplies for the Forest Service up to the fire tower on Satulah. John Wesley Edwards was the firewatcher and said that they had to carry the supplies up most of the way. Charles only weighed about 125 pounds at the time and couldn't see that he would do much good carrying all the supplies. So he asked John Edwards about driving up to the top and was told that it couldn't be done. They made one trip in the truck, and no one believed that they had done it. He did say that the drive back down was pretty scary.

Well, what did the CCC do in Highlands? First off, Charles said that the organization didn't build the Highlands School Auditorium, as we had been told. That was done by another of FDR's programs, the WPA, or Works Progress Administration (sometimes called "We Putter Around"). But it did do reforestation, road erosion control and other similar projects. Its workers built Van Hook Campground and Ammons Campground and developed the trail down to Dry Falls for the Forest Service.

We remember the erosion control on US 64 between Franklin and Cashiers. The bare banks on the new road were easy to wash out, and so they drove stakes in horizontal lines along the banks and laid what could be described as large strips of lath above each line of stakes. Charles added that they went down to Professor Harbison's place on the Walhalla Road and pulled up honeysuckle vines, which they then planted in the framework of stakes and lath that they had constructed.

Charles acquired another nickname while he was in Horse Cove. Most if not all of the young men, except for the LEMs, were from cities and had never been in the country. One day, while traveling back to camp in his Buick, he spotted a large rattlesnake sunning himself on a rock. So he took a shoelace from his boot, made a small loop in it and then cut a branch with a fork at the end. I think you are ahead of us. He caught the snake just below the head, lassoed it around the neck, put it in a burlap sack and carried it on to camp. You can imagine first the fright and then the curiosity that he caused. He got a piece of meat and let the snake strike it to show the venom from the fangs. Well, I am sure you have guessed his new nickname: "Snake."

Some of the local men in the camp were Van Frazier, Cecil Baldwin, Claude Houston, Jim Lowe, Pete Moses and Irwin Patton. Some of our local young ladies married men from the camp, including Bernice Baty, Mattie Lou Elliot, Grace Elliot, Betsy Potts, Jenny Keener, Ethel Shockley and Bernice Rice. Bernice Rice married Jim Lowe.

On a personal level, Dr. E.R. Gilbert, Isabel's grandfather, was the dentist in Highlands at the time. Looking through his "Dentist's Ledger," she found a number of CCC patients from Rome and Atlanta, Georgia, and Charlotte, North Carolina, and other towns in the South. Most of the work done was extractions, but in Dr. Gilbert's records there is a letter from the army at Fort McPherson denying a charge for a root canal. Apparently, the army wouldn't go for that procedure. Fillings back then were four dollars and extractions were five.

WHO MAINTAINED OUR ROADS BACK WHEN?

"Morning Sam. How's the family?"

"Just fine, Professor Harbison."

"Tom came by yesterday and got his check. Have you got any bills for me today Sam?"

"Yep, a big one: twenty-two dollars and thirty-five cents. Can you handle that, Professor?"

Professor Thomas G. Harbison looked at the time and amounts on the bills that Sam Calloway had given him. He added the figures and then wrote a check to S.L. Calloway for the amount and handed it to Sam. The date was June 27, 1913, and the payment was for work done on the Buck Creek Road.

For seven years, Professor Harbison served on the Macon County Road Commission. His job was to receive county road tax receipts allocated for road maintenance in the Flats and Highlands Townships and disburse them to the individuals that did the maintenance. (Some of you have probably heard of this man of many talents, and we will be hearing more about him this year. It seems that the State of North Carolina will be recognizing his many accomplishments in the form of a historic road marker, but let's get back to our county roads system and how it was managed back in the early part of the twentieth century.)

Road maintenance had been left up to the counties, but in 1915 the state established the first Highway Commission. You may remember that at that time automobiles were just becoming popular and affordable. A seven-member commission was formed that included the governor of the state. The commission in turn hired an engineer to provide technical assistance to county road–building efforts.

So who was involved in our part of the county? Well, let's turn to the ledgers that Professor Harbison kept: A.C. "Gus" Holt, Myron Russell, H.B. James and Frank Talley maintained the Scaly Road, along with Chester N. and Will Wright and Even Owens.

It appears that the Shortoff Road had mostly Wrights looking after it. There were C.N., Will, Henry, W.T. and George Wright, as well as Jack Henry, Jack Talley and Will Hicks. Ed, A.J. and John Picklesimer looked after the Walhalla Road along with Jabe Prater and C.N. and Will Wright.

Horse Cove Road was taken care of by M.D. Edwards, H.L. Hawkins and J.F. Talley. The new Franklin Road, which was probably the old

Walhalla Road, leading to Highlands.

Lamb Mountain Road and now called Flat Mountain Road, had many familiar names: S.L. Calloway, Maiden Keener, Roy Phillips, Ben Keener, Simon Speed, Frank Vinson and the Webbs, including George, W.M. and Joe Webb.

S.L. "Sam" Calloway and brother Tom Calloway are all that are recorded for the maintenance of the Buck Creek Road. And J.W. and R.P. McCall looked after the Nat Ridge Road and the Old Satulah Road.

Butler Jenkins was the only man paid for work on the Old Franklin Road. We're not sure where that was. Although Butler was a neighbor of ours from the 1930s through the 1960s, back during the period we are discussing he lived down on Walhalla Road. Finally, David McCall maintained the Turtle Pond Road.

We're not sure if this is of interest to most of our readers, but we hope that the relatives of these men will appreciate this bit of history.

The payments to these gentlemen were not much for the work that was done. The total for the fiscal years 1913 through 1919 was $8,435.06, for an average of $1,200.00 per year. According to the ledgers, Professor Harbison would sometimes advance his own money to pay for the work before the next year's tax receipts came to him.

There is a page in one of the ledgers covering tools and blasting materials. For the years 1913 to 1915, the total paid out was $159.63. As far as the records show, there was no provision for gravel. From the accompanying picture taken on the Walhalla Road, you can see what happened to the roads in rainy weather. Now imagine the same road in the winter. Tudor N. Hall related a story about coming up the Walhalla Road in the winter when the ruts were frozen. Trying to keep in the right ruts was like a train going down the track with the switch ahead half open. Many times if you used the wrong ruts, a wheel could be pulled off, or, at worst, the entire axle could come off.

Several years after Professor Harbison's records ended, in 1921, the State of North Carolina began its own highway-building program. The legislature transferred control of 5,500 miles of county roads, primarily roads that connected county seats, to the new State Highway Commission. Later in 1931, during the Great Depression, it took the remaining county roads into the state system and abolished existing county road commission.

One aspect that we remember from the late 1940s harkened back to the old county road maintenance days: the enormous rock outcropping located in the middle of the Buck Creek Road near the present recycling center. Cars and trucks had to drive on one side or the other to get by the rock. Requests and petitions to the State Highway Commission to get rid of the rock were ignored. So William "Bill" Way and Sam Baty took it as a challenge and dynamited the rock themselves.

The research for this section was taken from the pages of Professor Harbison's ledgers and from the NCDOT Board of Transportation History. The Harbison granddaughters, Ann Harbison, Christina Harbison Newton and Jessie Harbison Sheldon, loaned them to us until the archives area in the Old Hudson Library, a part of the Highlands Historical Society Historic Village, opened. They are available for researchers along with other old records and documents.

A SHORT HISTORY OF THE CHURCH OF THE INCARNATION

The magnificent new church building and sanctuary that you see today on Main Street is the culmination of 124 years of Episcopal worship in

Highlands. Beginning in 1876, Reverend John Archibald Deal was called to minister in Western North Carolina. First living in Murphy and later in Cartoogechaye near Franklin, he brought the word. His first service in Highlands was held on October 30, 1879, in a small building at the corner of Second and Main Streets also being used for a school and community meetings. This was five years after the town was founded in 1875.

Our history of the area tells us that Sarah Whiteside Norton, the first white child born in Whiteside Cove, was the daughter of Barak Norton and Mary Nicholson. She was brought into a family who worshipped in the Anglican faith. Before that her Norton ancestors were Quakers who emigrated from Ireland. So it is no surprise that two descendants of Barak and Mary, David Norton and Jeremiah Pierson, were some of the founders of the Church of the Incarnation. In 1894, they, along with Doctor Henry T. O'Farrell, were petitioners to form a mission. In addition, Tudor Tucker Hall and Meta Norton Frost were also petitioners.

Mr. Hall donated the money to purchase the property at the corner of Fifth and Main Streets from the Rideout family, and in 1895, a contract was let to build a church. In 1896, the church was completed and consecrated by Bishop Joseph B. Cheshire. Reverend Deal continued as priest-in-charge until 1906 or 1907. His duties extended to churches at Highlands, Franklin, Cartoogechaye and Cashiers. He accomplished this mostly on horseback and by presiding over services on a rotation basis approximately every fourth Sunday.

The present church was built to accommodate about one hundred people. It took about fifty years or so to come close to filling the church even in the summer. As a mission, Incarnation could not support a full-time priest and was dependant on the bishop of the diocese to provide priests on a part-time basis to be shared with other churches. But in the summer, the Episcopal Church Women organization took the initiative to seek out priests for one month at a time. This is where the tradition of Silver Teas began. Held in various members' homes, the money raised went for many things, including supply priests. There are over forty priests listed in the Church's First Hundred Years history book who filled these part-time posts. One of them was Reverend Robb White Jr. from Thomasville, Georgia, in 1928. He just missed marrying Isabel's parents by one month. Another supply minister who came in 1926 from Charleston, South Carolina, was Reverend William Way, whose son, William Way Jr., married Tony's mother. Isabel Robertson remembers Reverend Way as "mean Willy," which is another story.

An early photo of the Episcopal Church of the Incarnation.

For some ten years from 1931 to 1940, there were two part-time, year-round priests, including Horace Duncan's father, former parishioner Reverend Norvin Duncan, and Reverend Frank Bloxham. Then, in 1940, Reverend A. Rufus Morgan became our rector and served until 1955. He lived in Franklin and had an even larger charge, going all the way to Murphy and Cherokee. Dr. Morgan trained layman to conduct services in his absence. The next minister was Dr. Herbert Koepp-Baker, who came to Highlands to teach at Western Carolina University. He was trained as a clinical psychologist and a speech therapist, in addition to being an ordained Episcopal priest. He had sufficient income, so he accepted the post at Incarnation as the first full-time, year-round rector for a nominal sum. By 1958, he had convinced the vestry and Bishop M. George Henry that Incarnation was ready to be a self-supporting parish.

The first expansion was made during the last years of Dr. Morgan's tenure. A combination parish hall/kitchen and a bathroom were added on to the north side of the sanctuary, and the partition wall was removed between the two. So on Sundays, bi-fold doors were opened and extra seating was

The interior of the church circa 1940s.

provided for about twenty-five people. Later, during Reverend Gale Webbe's tenure (1960–71), the church built a rondette behind the northeast corner for a Sunday school. From that period through the 1970s, there were as many as twenty or more children in Sunday school classes in the summer in the rondette. Reverend Fred Hovey was rector from 1972 to 1978.

In the early 1980s, during the tenure of Reverend Charles Bryan (1979–94), a two-story addition was added onto the northeast side of the church, which included a new parish hall and kitchen along with Sunday school rooms on the ground floor underneath. It was then that a parishioner disassembled the rondette and moved it to Horse Cove. For the first time, the church now had a place for offices in the former parish hall, and the wall between the two was closed back. Two and then three services began in the summer season.

During the late eighties and into the mid-nineties, there were several proposals for church expansion. At that time, the congregation filled the sanctuary at both the nine and eleven o'clock services in the summer. Something had to be done to plan for the next one hundred years. A future planning committee had been meeting for some ten or more years, and finally a proposal was made to build a new sanctuary rather than enlarge the original. What you see today is the culmination of the start of the second century at Incarnation: a large sanctuary that will seat over 250 people, room for the choir, an enlarged parish hall and kitchen, more Sunday school rooms, a library, a vestry meeting room, several offices, a workroom and lastly a meeting room that can used by various organizations in the community. A recent survey completed by the National Church in New York came to the attention of those at Incarnation. It listed Incarnation in the top ten in percentage of growth of all Episcopal parishes in the United States. This additional growth came during the period of 1995–2003 under the leadership of Reverend Michael Jones.

Currently Reverend Steve Hines is serving as interim rector while the church is conducting a search for a new rector. Steve is no stranger to Highlands or Incarnation. During his seminary years, he served under Reverend Bryan in youth ministry. He also was rector of the Church of the Good Shepherd in Cashiers for a number of years. His name may be familiar to Episcopalians as he is the son of former bishop John Hines. Our current rector is Reverend Brian Sullivan.

Over the last one hundred years or more, there have been six descendants and spouses of descendants of the founders, who have served as junior wardens, senior wardens or both. One of the longest serving of the descendants was Tudor Norton Hall. He served as warden, as well as sexton, during the later mission years. He then served as senior warden in the early parish years for a total of thirty years. Many more descendants have served on the vestry itself. Now there are fifth-, sixth-, seventh- and eighth-generation descendants of the founders that call Incarnation home.

ABRAHAM LINCOLN SLEPT HERE

Well, maybe. No one knows for sure. This is not a new story—Abraham Lincoln's paternity, that is. No, it has been around for almost two hundred years. But what does that have to do with this section?

In Ridpath's *With the World's People*, the author defines the difference between history and tradition: "The first rests on the testimony of witnesses contemporary with the fact described; the latter reposes on the testimony of those who were removed in time and place, or both, from the circumstances and events constituting the subject matter of the story."

We all know that history states that Abraham Lincoln was born in Kentucky...or is it tradition? We learned in school that his parents were Tom or Thomas Lincoln and Nancy Hanks. The family later moved to Indiana and then to Illinois. Ever since he became a national figure, stories have come out of Virginia, North Carolina, South Carolina and Kentucky about his parents and particularly his father.

Many authors have done exhaustive research into where Tom Lincoln and Nancy Hanks were born, raised, met and married. The problem is that all these authorities and biographers have a different slant on the main characters, his parents. A number of the written accounts list from nine to sixteen candidates as Abraham Lincoln's father. These include Martin Hardin of Kentucky, the adopted son of Chief Justice John Marshall, the father of Jefferson Davis, John C. Calhoun, Abraham Inlow (or Enloe) and others. Even with the name "Inlow" and "Enloe" there are four men who are alleged to have been Lincoln's father. In Kentucky alone, there appear to have been a number of men with the name Thomas Lincoln. In the particular states in question, there were as many as *ten* Nancy Hankses. The most popular candidates for father of Abraham, besides Tom Lincoln, are Abraham Enloe and John C. Calhoun.

Your authors are not going to take any side in this continuing argument. Rather we would like to take these two candidates off the shelf and give you two different authors' positions. According to Judge Felix Eugene Alley, son of Sarah Whiteside Norton and Colonel John Alley, in his book *Random Thoughts and Musings of a Mountaineer*, John C. Calhoun is the most logical person to have fathered Abraham Lincoln. The story begins in Abbeville County, South Carolina. John C. Calhoun returned there in 1807 after finishing the study of law in Connecticut. He would make frequent trips to Pendleton, South Carolina, in the Pendleton district, for his law practice. Between Pendleton and Abbeville was the small town of Craytonville, where he and his colleagues would stop for the night at a tavern owned by Ann Hanks. He became interested in an attractive barmaid by the name of Nancy Hanks. Nature took its course, and Nancy found herself pregnant. Obviously this put Calhoun in a predicament. Being named the father of the child of a barmaid would ruin him socially and politically.

According to Hanks family accounts at the time, John C. met up with an itinerant drover who worked from time to time for Calhoun and others. His name was Tom Lincoln. Lincoln was planning to travel to Kentucky, and John C. hired Lincoln to carry Nancy to her uncle's home in Kentucky. On the way, they stopped at his sometime employer Abe Enloe's house in the Oconaluftee area of Western North Carolina, where Nancy Hanks gave birth to a son, Abraham Lincoln, in a log cabin. After the birth, Enloe paid Tom Lincoln to carry on to Kentucky, as Mrs. Enloe was very suspicious of her husband. He, too, had traveled through South Carolina as a drover of pigs and cattle. So Tom and Nancy continued on to Kentucky, where they were married.

James Cathey, in his book *The Genesis of Lincoln*, provides a different scenario. Mrs. Enloe needed a servant and contacted her relatives in Rutherford, North Carolina. They in turn sent Nancy Hanks. It came about that Nancy became pregnant, allegedly by Mr. Enloe. When the child was born, Mrs. Enloe became very upset. So, as the story goes, Abraham Enloe paid Tom Lincoln, one of his employees, to take Nancy and the baby out of the country. On the way through Tennessee and Kentucky, the child was named after his real father Abraham and his adoptive father Lincoln.

Now what does this have to do with Highlands? The present owner of a log cabin here in Highlands tells the story of the origin of his home. A neighbor told him a story that he had heard from his wife's grandfather. Several years later, the homeowner met John Parris, the columnist and vice-president of the *Asheville-Citizen Times*, who corroborated the story that the log cabin here in Highlands could have been owned by Abraham Enloe, and the cabin was moved to Highlands from the Oconaluftee area of Cherokee, North Carolina.

The truth of either of these stories cannot be proven. Even if the cabin was once owned by Abraham Enloe, who is to say that he or John C. Calhoun was the father of Abraham Lincoln? Both Cathey and Alley claim to have accounts contemporary of the time, but is it history or tradition? The real truth comes when you are sitting by the fireplace of that old log cabin and recount what could have been. And does it make any difference?

Recently a descendant of the Enloe family, Dave Enloe, and his wife, Kathleen, made a trip all the way from their home in California to visit the cabin. MaryAnn Sloan called me when they stopped at the Hudson Library for directions to the cabin. I didn't consider the significance of the request until the next morning when I passed the cabin. There was a couple standing in the yard of the cabin, and we stopped to see if by chance this was the couple MaryAnn had called us about. We had a nice chat with them, and they told us that they had stopped on the way here at Cherokee to find the grave of Abraham Enloe. They were directed to a cemetery at Oconaluftee and did find his grave. We compared sources of information and each of us provided the other with what we had.

History and Other Interesting Vignettes of Highlands

ARMISTICE DAY, NOVEMBER 11, 1918

"In Flanders Fields the poppies blow, between the crosses row on row"—this from a poem written by Lieutenant Colonel John McCrae, MD, in the Canadian army during a lull in the Great War. He wrote it while sitting on an ambulance near Ypres, looking across at the cemetery. Isabel remembers having to memorize the poem in school. Some of you may remember World War I veterans selling paper poppies on the anniversary of the end of the war. We thought it would be proper to honor our veterans on Veterans Day who are buried in Highlands Memorial Park:

Alstaetter, Frederrick 1875/1966 Col. USA WWI
Anderson 80th Ohio Union
Bailey, Henry "Hank"
Baldwin, Robert G. 12-13-01/3-24-49
Baldwin, Robert Lee, Jr. 4-8-55/4-21-93 USN Viet
Baty, Clarence USN WWII
Baty, Earl USN WWII
Baty, Edward J. "Buzz" 7-10-20/11-1-06 USN WWII
Baty, Homer D. 11-12-22/5-24-94 Pfc. USA WWII
Baty, Harry 11-22-13/4-20-52 Pvt. USMC WWII
Baty, James 1-10-22/4-7-42 Pfc. USAAF WWII
Baty, John USMC WWII
Baty, Ronald USMC WWII
Baty, William H. "Joe" 6-26-15/7-7-84 USA WWII
Beal, Robert I. 4-6-1892/10-21-54 Pvt. USA WWI
Beal, George 12-24-15/5-25-44 FA USA WWII
Beale, John E.
Beale, Harry 7-7-21/1-17-91 Pfc. USMC WWII
Binford, Thomas E. 6-20-00/6-12-87 Col. USA WWII
Brockway, Jack W. 11-28-13/7-10-95 OSS WWII
Bryson, Walter A. 11-14-1890/10-6-1983 WWI
Bryson, W.N., Jr. "Ned"4-27-47/3-9-99 USA Viet
Burnette, John D. 3-25-1896/3-1-1984 Cpl. USA WWI
Caziarc, Elliot 4-5-1877/12-1-1959 Col. USA SAW WWI
Calloway, John Morris 11-20-27/9-25-68 WO USNR WWII
Calloway, Tudor Sam D. 8-17-17/8-28-80 WWII
Chalker, Albert L. 2-27-26/10-26-04 USA WWII

Highlands Cemetery.

Chambers, Overton S. 5-17-1899/10-2-1977 USA Ambul. WWI

Chastain, Carl 9-29-1926/3-23-1995 USAAC WWII

Chastain, Charles Henry 2-24-1919/5-24-1988 WWII

Chastain, Oscar E. 5-7-1913/7-18-88 Sgt. USA WWII Korea

Cleaveland, Carlton 10-11-1921/8-17-1972 USCG WWII

Cole, Betty 8-18-09/10-25-76 MSgt. USMC WWII

Cook, Chester W., Sr. 10-28-1896/11-27-1984 Lt. Col. USA WWI
    and WWII

Connatser, Roy 6-30-10/7-1-76 USN

Cook, Frank B. 9-3-1892/9-18-89 WWI

Cooper, Madge 8-2-04/1-6-90 MSgt. USA WWII

Corn, Hollan J. 8-27-1913/9-17-1989 USAAC WWII Korea

Crain, Albert 8-12-1924/10-20-1942 US Coast Artillery

Crane. Clarence L. 6-4-26/3-14-94

Crawford, James 7-21-19/10-5-82 USN WWII

Creswell, Ligon T. 2-21-28/7-9-94 Pvt. USA Korea

Crisp, Doug A. 5-31-47/3-18-97 USMC Viet

Crisp, Willard 1920/1979 WWII

Crunkleton, Carl Newton 9-14-18/7-17-46 USA WWII

Crunkleton, Seth H. 5-14-1875/10-18-49 Cpl. Coast Artil. WWI

Crunkleton, Thomas L. 9-12-15/9-10-56 TEC USA WWII

Crunkleton, I. Tolliver 1913/1971 WWII

Davis, James Albert 1-13-28/1-9-03 USN WWII

Day, Emory F. 6-20-1891/3-20-1967 USA WWI

Duke, Albert A. 9-2-21/12-26-76 USN WWII

Dunken, Morris M. 7-16-1922/7-18-1985 USN WWII

Durgin, John "Pat" 1844/1939 Sgt. 10ᵗʰ NH Union army Civil Scout US 7ᵗʰ Cav. Indian Wars

Dwyer, William "Bill" 1907/1987 WWII

Edwards, Louis A. 5-15-05/12-27-99 Lt. USA WWII

Flemming, Frank 6-25-1921/5-25-1979 Lt. USA WWII

Fuller, Pope 4-12-16/7-31-79 Maj. USA WWII

Gibson, Charlie C. 6-6-23/12-10-99 USA WWII

Gordon, John 3-11-1930/6-4-1985 USMC Korea

Grover, Edward M. 1-9-11/8-18-87 Capt. USAAF WWII

Ford, James R. 1908/1978 Sgt. USA WWII

Hall, Tudor T. 1844/1918 Pvt. Hvy Art. CSA Civil

Hall, Tudor G. 10-22-32/11-3-92 USA

Harrell, W. Jackson 11-19-15/7-16-95 WWII

Harrison, Richard M. 7-24-1890/8-15-75 WWI

Hathaway, Allen E. 12-8-1927/2-13-2000 WWII

Heacock, Johnathan 41ˢᵗ Iowa Inf. Civil

Hedden, Henry H. 7-21-22/5-21-72 SSgt. USAAF WWII

Hedden, J. Quincy 1898/1957 WWI

Hedden, Preleau 11-13-1896/8-18-1987 WWI

Henderson, John E. 12-13-19/5-3-97 WWII

Henry, Claud A., Sr. 8-18-24/12-13-04 USA WWII

Henry, Roosevelt John 6-3-22/2-14-68 Pvt. USA WWII

Henry, Sam F. 1914/1978 USA WWII

Henriques, C.B. 5-25-07/5-5-03 Capt. USN WWII

Herring, Gene 2-19-28/9-21-81 Col. USA WWII Korea

Hicks, John C.

Hicks, Lawrence

Hines, James A.

Hodges, J.A. 8-12-1892/5-22-1982 WWI

Hodges, Christy A. 1-13-1924/4-28-74 USMC WWII

Holt, Harry A., Jr. 1931/1984

Hooper, Robert E. 7-4-20/7-7-85 TEC USA WWII

Hopper, Bobby 12-13-33/7-15-88 Sm. USN WWII

House, James

Houston, Richard T. 1933/1998 USA Korea

Jenkins, Roscoe 9-12-21/9-11-93 TEC USA WWII

Jones, Joseph M. 9-11-1891/9-10-63 WWI

Keener, James Donald 1-18-27/10-2-83 WWII

Keener, Joseph B. 11-8-10/9-8-03 USA WWII

Kelly, Frank A. 1-13-19/2-8-94 Capt. USAAC WWII

Lambert, George 10-20-11/6-6-80 WWII

Lonabarger, Robert E. 1-2-19/10-24-79 WWII USA

McCall, V.W. "Bill" 5-17-24/10-16-96 USA WWII

McCall, Robert Michael 6-21-49/5-16-02 USA Viet

McClure, George Pratt 4-22-15/12-14-86 Pvt. USA WWII

McConnell, G. Robert "Bobby" 4-13-1899/5-1-77 USA WWI

McDonough, Andrew F. 11-13-27/10-12-99 WWII

McKinney, Elmer

McKinney, James 1919/1978 Sgt. USA WWII

McKinney, Thomas G. 5-4-18/5-4-78 WWII

Mangum, Dr. C.T. 1921/1996 US Army Medical Corps

Massey, Joe A. 6-13-07/9-21-89 TEC USA WWII

Matthews, Dr. W.A. 10-31-11/3-28-72 USA WWII

Misner, Leslie 12-27-1887/2-14-78 WWI

Moore, Robert L. 9-8-09/3-18-67 Pfc. FA USA WWII

Munger, Herbert Leslie 5-20-25/11-21-87 Cox USN WWII

Nall, W.C. "Billy" 1-25-20/7-3-95 Capt. USAAC CBI

Nettles, Ervin 7-17-20/1-17-94 Sgt. USAAC WWII

Norton, Charlie Ray "Bo" 6-21-32/6-15-58 Cpl. MP USA

Norton, David 1835/1912 Lt. CSA Civil

Norton, Ray E. 6-26-1892/3-11-1953 USA FA WWI

Oxford, C. Dixon 1914/1998

Patten, Richard 8-8-30/1-22-01 Korea

Paul, Charles W., Sr. 8-16-14/1-7-82 SSgt. USA WWII

Perry, John H.C. 8-28-1891/9-1-64 USA Ambul. WWI

Pierson, Kendall 10-30-17/10-23-99 WWII

Pierson, Val S. 1-14-20/12-24-71 Lt. Col. USA WWII Korea

Pierson, William K. 5-3-55/9-9-74 USA

Pierson, W.P. "Bill" 10-29-11/3-8-90.

Porterfield, Herbert D. 7-5-1887/6-3-1969 Col. USA WWI

Potts, Edward 1-14-18/4-12-92 Sgt. USA WWII

Potts, John Steven 7-30-21/1-18-99 USA WWII

Potts, John Stephen 1825/1910 Civil

Potts, Richard D. 11-17-32/11-13-03 Cpl. USA Korea

Potts, Roy E. 2-10-25/12-21-89 MAM 2 USN WWII

Potts, Willis Leon "Deadeye" 11-22-26/8-8-01 WWII

Potts, William Robert 11-26-11/1-4-73 WWII

Potts, William R. "Bill" 10-10-33/9-13-67

Reese, Carey L. 10-21-16/6-12-81 S2 USN WWII

Reese, Coleman 4-19-20/2-9-05 Sgt. USA WWII

Reese, Howard W. "Bob" 12-28-09/5-13-90 S2 USN WWII

Reese, James Norman 1931/9-11-2005 USAF Korea

Reese, Joseph W., Jr. 11-5-07/5-14-99 USA WWII

Rhodes, Robert L. 10-13-1913/3-14-01 LCDR USN WWII

Rice, Lewis

Rice, Luther W., Jr. 6-26-15/7-17-68 FA USA WWII

Rice, William Herbert "Cub" USCG WWII

Richert, Marguerite L. 9-15-04/8-6-71 Capt. Nurse USA WWII

Rideout, James E. 1872/1901 SAW

Rippetoe, Frances Joe Hedden 5-15-28/5-19-01 SSgt. USAF

Rogers, Bert Monroe 4-21-39/6-25-91 USA

Rogers, Birtie B. 2-20-1893/11-13-22 USA WWI

Rogers, Arthur D., Sr. 9-5-20/2-12-67 Pfc. ORD WWII

Rogers, Arthur D. "Spec," Jr. 6-22-43/2-23-01 SP USA Viet

Russell, Elaine Trott 9-20-24/9-28-02

Russell, James D., Sr. 11-17-07/12-21-70 Pvt. USA WWII

Russell, William T. 8-20-24/2-25-00 Lt. Col. USA WWII Korea Viet

Saussy, George 1-6-1898/9-27-64 Sgt. USA WWI

Schowalter, Roy R. 9-14-1897/3-14-86 Pvt. USA WWI

Sellers, Edgar P. 10-26-27/11-8-88 USN WWII

Sevigny, Albert, Jr. 7-25-35/9-16-94 USMC Korea

Shattuck, Warren, Sr. 1906/1981 WWII

Shouse James E. 5-18-07/7-29-96 USA WWII

Shockley, Frank Edwin 10-20-27/6-12-71 USA WWII

Shuler, Glenn A. 6-15-14/3-25-93 Sgt. USAAC WWII

Simmons, Wilbur 11-1-29/11-25-93 WWII

Sledge, Lamar Cobb 1-8-05/8-10-72 Cav. USA WWII

Speed, Harold E. 1-13-27/10-28-93 Cpl. USAAC WWII

Speed, Thomas Simon 3-24-1894/3-2-61 Pvt. USA WWI

Stewart, Fred H. 1894/1989 USA WWI

Stewart, Fred, Jr. 4-6-27/3-8-01 USA WWII

Stewart, Jimmy 7-8-47/5-20-02 Sgt. USAF Viet

St. Germain, Raymond 4-12-58/4-22-02 USCG

Sullivan, Claude T. 5-1-08/6-17-70 WWII

Talley, Carter E. 2-9-13/2-23-81 Pvt. USA WWII

Talley, Richard E. 1-27-36/7-7-78 HH1 USN Viet

Thompson, Magnus S. "Bud" 4-9-26/9-28-88 Sgt. USA WWII

Thornton, Burwell W. 5-18-1897/8-22-76 Sgt. USA WWI

Todd, David 10-19-11/12-1-02 Lt. Col. USAAC WWII

Traylor, Forest l., Jr. 11-2-18/3-25-87 Lt. USA WWII

Walden, Paul C. 4-29-13/7-29-76 USA WWII

Waller, Lindal 2-9-31/7-22-99

Waldon, Theron D. 1-18-1838/12-12-1906 Union 72nd NY Vol.

Watson, Walter L. 8-8-1894/2-7-1969 Eng. 1 USN WWI

Webb, Ed 5-20-09/8-4-50 USCG WWII

Wiley, Calvin Floyd 8-9-1914/3-1-2000 USA WWII

Wiley, David Erskin 1917/1972 WWII

Wilson, Curt A. 2-18-18/8-14-72 USN WWII

Wilson, Duane 3-26-27/4-19-80 Sgt. USA WWII

Wilson, Gordon 12-8-31/7-9-94 Capt. USAF Korea Viet

Wright, Chester N. 2-16-17/2-18-83 WWII

Wright, Henry 1-22-1893/6-2-1983 WWI

Zachary, Carl "Bud" 3-25-20/11-23-94 USA WWII

Zachary, Claude 1-21-18/12-19-93 USA WWII

Zachary, Lloyd 1926/1983 USA WWII

Zenick, John J. 12-19-11/12-29-89 Pfc. USA WWII

Zoellner, Carl H.10-11-1890/9-8-1978 USA WWI

Zoellner, Wm. Henry 4-20-1929/4-8-45 Sgt. USA WWII Buried Margraten U.S. Military Cemetery, Holland

Abbreviations: CBI—China Burma India Theatre; CSA—Confederate States of America; FA—Field Artillery; SAW—Spanish American War; Sm—Seaman; USA—Army; USAF—Air Force; USAAF—Army Air Corps; USCG—Coast Guard; USMC—Marine Corps; USN—Navy; Viet—Vietnam.

Please let us know of any other veterans so we may add to the above information.

END OF AN ERA: CRANE'S RIDING STABLES

The morning was cool, and the breath of the horses hung in the air around their nostrils. Most of the children were dressed in blue jeans and wool shirts as they stood around the muddy stable yard watching as bridles and saddles were fitted on the horses. Several parents stood in the background, possibly hesitant if their child had never ridden a horse. One by one, the experienced and novice riders were helped onto their own horse. The youngest boy glanced back at his parents as his horse was led off by a guide holding the reins.

This scene was repeated over and over throughout the summers starting in the early 1930s in various rented fields, stable yards and barnyards all over Highlands. Back then, there were at least three riding stables in town. The scene continued every summer until 1999, when Crane's Stables closed.

Let's go back to those days. The names of the stable owners that come to mind are Simon Speed, Levi and Frank Crane and George S. Cubbedge's Sa-Hi Stables. Experienced riders could take out horses on their own, as was the case with livery stables that flourished earlier in Highlands. But inexperienced and younger riders were sent out with a guide, and usually a guide went along with a group. Back then the rate was one dollar per hour, or you could get a season pass.

Simon Speed worked out of the stables at Highlands Country Club, although at one time both Frank Crane and Speed were there together. The Cranes usually used a barn literally situated in the middle of Second Street, below the Zoellner's home, between Main and Spring Streets. On occasion, they used a field at the corner of Fifth and Chestnut Streets. George Cubbedge would use the Zoellner barn, as well as another barn belonging to Helen Wilson, near the dance hall along First Street.

The actual location of the stables, where the horses were kept at night, varied. The Cranes' horses were ridden back at night to the Crane farm on Oak Street. Frank Crane tore down the original barn that Levi built in 1926–27, just below the two-story home, in the late 1960s. That was after he built a new barn across Oak Street from the old barn and house. This is the property purchased recently for the future site of the Bascom Fine Arts Center.

Simon Speed kept his horses at the club at night and would ride, along with his son Sanford, back and forth to his home off Buck Creek Road. Betty Speed Wood explained that her Uncle Simon rode back and forth

The Levi Crane family.

on what is now Myrtle Speed Road, across to Flat Mountain Road, over to Billy Cabin Road, winding through Cullasaja Heights to the Franklin Road and up to Cobb Road and the stables. We remember Simon as a thin, nattily dressed man in riding jodhpurs and boots, khaki shirt and a type of campaign hat. When Isabel asked Betty Speed Wood if she rode her uncle's horses, she said she rode her grandmother's mule. In talking with Chuck Crane, Frank Crane's nephew, he said he would shoe Simon Speed's horses at the club after he got off work on the greenskeeper crew. According to Oscar F Crane, other men that shod horses in Highlands were Albert Patterson, Joe Jenkins and his brother, Clarence Crane.

Marilyn Cubbedge Manley told us about her father, George Cubbedge, who owned Sa-Hi Riding Academy in Savannah. They had a summer home that they bought from Margaret Young, on the backside of Satulah, as well as a barn and some pasture. Each morning and night, the Cubbedges—father, daughter and son George—would lead the horses down to town passing Charlie Anderson's house as they turned onto Spring Street and over to whichever barn they had rented for the summer. After bringing his horses to Highlands for a number of years, he began taking them to Camp Merrie-Woode.

Crane's Stables.

In talking with year-round and summer people, there were various stories of these stables and their owners. My sister Sarah got a job currying Si Stannard's personal horses, which he didn't rent. Anne Major Doggett, who lived across the street from us, and Sarah were the only children he let ride. He didn't like boys, so for an entire summer Lewis Doggett, Anne's boyfriend back then, sat on the fence while Anne and Sarah rode. Mr. Stannard had a mean dog that he kept chained up on a little island in the small stream that went through the property. Over the summer, Lewis got to know the dog well. Near the end of the summer, he asked Mr. Stannard if he could ride a horse. Stannard allowed that if Lewis—he called him "boy"—could pet his dog, he could ride. Lewis walked through the stream, picked up the mean dog in his arms and got to ride with Anne and Sarah.

Another humorous incident happened when Anne's grandmother took in a number of children from Anderson, South Carolina, during the polio summer of 1946. In addition to those children, there were a number of others from Florida staying at Highlands Inn. Anne thought it would be a good idea to take all of them horseback riding. She approached Mr. Cubbedge about getting horses for about two dozen friends one afternoon. His only question was "Do they know how to ride?" Anne had no idea but told him that they did. The ride was for one hour, and near the end, with Anne leading, the horses were ready to head home. Most of the children were on horseback for the first time, and either someone decided to break into a canter or the horses were just ready to head for the barn, but a mad rush began near Lindenwood Lake. One of the first to pass Anne was a boy by the name of Inman Mays, who was dressed rather comically in ballet slippers and a cape. As he rode by Anne, he shouted, "He won't throw me!" According to Anne, only three of the group arrived back at Cubbedge's on horseback: the others had fallen off at some point between Lindenwood Lake and the stables. One more incident that comes to mind was when Julianne Russell, who owned her own horse, was cited by the Highlands police chief (back then there was only one policeman) for riding on the sidewalk downtown. Isabel's grandfather, Dr. E.R. Gilbert, was cited for the same offense a number of years earlier.

On another occasion, my sister Sarah and Anne took all of Simon Speed's horses from town out to his pasture off Flat Mountain Road. It took them most of the day to do this, and Anne said that they were very tired when they got home. Tony didn't ride very much, but if he did usually it was at Crane's. He can remember one time when he was riding beside Main Street back to the barn; he thinks he may have been cantering. The next thing he knew, he was on the ground, and the horse kept going. He looked up and saw a clothesline strung above him. Apparently somebody didn't like horseback riders. One of the perks at Crane's Stables was that they would bring horses to your home and pick you up.

According to Lassie Crane Buchanan, Frank Crane's daughter, and Oscar Crane, his son, both the grandchildren of Levi Butler Crane, Levi and his son Phil ran a freight line from Dillard, Georgia, to Highlands. Levi also hauled produce to and from Walhalla, South Carolina, as well as carrying the mail in and out of Highlands. He also had his own livery stable in Highlands. Frank joined his father in a new venture when they opened up Crane's Riding Stables in 1932. The business grew, and for a number of years they had eighteen to twenty horses. When Levi died, Frank continued the business with his sons, Clarence and Oscar, until his death in the mid-1970s. Oscar and Clarence continued the business until 1999, the year Clarence passed away.

Frank and Effie Miller Crane's home was on Oak Street near the Franklin Road. This is where Lassie's seven brothers and sister—Margaret, Frank M., Clarence, Robert, Carlton, Chester and Oscar—grew up. We asked her if she rode any of the horses. She said she never had time to ride after helping with all the household chores and looking after her brothers.

In talking with many of Isabel's contemporaries that grew up in town, there seems to have been more locals that rode at Crane's than any other stable, though there aren't any statistics available to support this. Anne Anderson Sellers said that she and two of her three sisters, Mary and Jane, rode at Crane's. Anne remembers her horse Fred, how Clarence taught her how to ride and how she graduated from a western saddle to an English saddle. Her sister Mary continues to ride to this day. Isabel and Sarah had season passes at Crane's, as did the Anderson sisters. Isabel liked to ride but wasn't interested the same way as Sarah.

The favorite trails were around Mirror Lake: across Mirror Lake over Billy Cabin and back; or up Big Bear Pen road to Upper Lake Road and from there to Bowery Road to Horse Cove Road and then back on Lower Lake Road past Lindenwood Lake down Chestnut to Fifth Street and home to Oak Street. If you were riding out of the stables at Highlands Country Club, you would ride around Cobb Road and then across to Mirror Lake and back or out the Dillard Road and down to Glen Falls and back. Many of the streets and roads were still gravel or dirt up to the late 1940s.

We have called this piece of Highlands' history "End of an Era" for the obvious reason that there are no longer any stables in or close to Highlands. Lucinda Jane Morgan Crane, Levi Butler Crane's second wife, bought the Crane property over eighty years ago from Thomas Fleming Parker and his second wife, Harriet Horry Frost Parker. This was part of a twenty-six-acre subdivision that Parker had purchased in the early 1900s. Thomas Fleming Parker's connection with Highlands goes back to the 1870s. His mother, Margaretta Amelia Fleming Parker, was widowed during the Civil War, and she remarried S. Prioleau Ravenel from Charleston. Briefly, Thomas F. Parker and stepfather Prioleau Ravenel supervised the construction of the First Presbyterian Church, to which his mother and aunt donated the bulk of the funds for the lot and construction. Parker also designed the pews and the first altar for the church. Later, he worked with S.T. Kelsey and his son, Harlan, at the Kelsey nursery in Highlands and managed the nursery after the Kelseys moved on to start another town and another nursery in Linville, North Carolina. In the early 1900s, Parker moved to Greenville, South Carolina, to start a textile mill and became a major civic leader there. He brought his friend Harlan Kelsey down to

Greenville from his home in Boxford, Massachusetts, to draft a city plan. Parker's first interest was the public library in Greenville.

So the end of the Crane Stable and horseback riding in Highlands becomes the start of a *new era* with the Bascom Center for the Visual Arts. The stable will be moved and begin a new life as the center for potters, with wheels and kilns. What was once the subdivision of civic-minded Thomas F. Parker, and then a farm and horse stable of the Crane family for almost seventy years, will now be a center for all of the visual arts in Highlands.

CADDYING AT HIGHLANDS COUNTRY CLUB

The mist had risen from the Firth of Forth as a group of men paused in their game. It was 1681, and the place was the Leith Links, an early golf course near Edinburgh, Scotland. The Duke of York had sponsored a tournament, and his young caddy was Andrew Dickson. This is the first mention of the word caddy in connection with the game of golf. Dickson went on to become an Edinburgh golf club maker.

One of the occupations that has passed into history, at least in Highlands, is the golf caddy. Since golf is mentioned as far back as the fifteenth century in Scotland and golf caddy since the seventeenth century, it has been a true and honorable profession. The word caddy or caddie is said to come from the French *le cadet*, meaning a boy. In eighteenth-century Scotland, it was a general term for porter or errand boy. So what was the job of the caddy? To begin with, there weren't any bags, so someone had to carry a bundle of clubs. The term became associated with the person that carried the clubs. Perhaps there were two caddies, as the word "forecaddy" was used to describe the caddy that was sent down the course to where the ball might land. Apparently, golf balls were more expensive than the pay of a caddy, thus the term now used is "fore" to signal that the golfer has teed off a ball. Isn't this all too interesting! But I thought it would help if we knew where it all started.

Highlands Estates, which became Highlands Country Club, was not the first golf course in Highlands. There were at least three that preceded it. Several were short-lived, and the last of three, the nine-hole course at the Hall House, lasted the longest, from about 1906 to the early 1930s. So let's begin with a young man, John "Pluck" Baty, who caddied at the Hall House and was one of the first to caddy at Highlands Country Club.

History and Other Interesting Vignettes of Highlands

For the sake of brevity, we'll use the term that everyone recognized in the old days—the "Club." Pluck and his family lived near the Hall House course. He started caddying there and then went out to the Club when it got started in the late 1920s. The Donald Ross–designed course was nine holes to begin with, and in 1930 it was extended to eighteen holes. I asked Pluck if he did "doubles" at the beginning, but he said that didn't happen until the back nine holes were completed. "Doubles" meant carrying two golf bags at a time. He and Henry Cleaveland were the first caddies to go around the finished eighteen-hole course. The caddy master at the beginning was Durand Wiley. The starting pay was fifty cents for nine holes and anywhere from ten cents to twenty-five cents for tips. Pluck's favorite player was Crawford Rainwater.

Our next caddy is Chuck Crane. He practically grew up at the Club. He recalls that he went with his father, Phillip Crane, to the course as a child of five or six. They lived down in Gold Mine, and when he first started working at the Club, he walked the entire way. He was possibly the caddy and later ground crew worker who walked the longest to work. He began caddying at age eleven and did this until he joined the ground crew. He caddied with some of the Reese brothers and Jim Munger. His pay back then was sixty-five cents per round of eighteen holes, with tips of twenty-five cents. He tried to get as many "doubles" as he could. The bags were smaller and lighter back then, not like the heavy leather ones with all the clubs that are used today. Scott Hudson and later Mr. Happoldtt hired men with pickup trucks to bring up boys from Franklin to caddy, sometimes as many as thirty or forty boys in one day. At that time, boys would also come from Satolah, Georgia. This was apparently an indication of how many more players were on the course than in Pluck Baty's early years. Chuck caddied for George Woodruff and V.Z. Rainwater. But his days as a caddy were short-lived. By age thirteen, he was hired on to the ground crew. Back then, the fairways were mowed by horses pulling gang reel mowers and the greens by push reel mowers. Even then, when he got through work at noon on Saturday, he might be called to caddy a round in the afternoon. He continued in that area and became head greenskeeper. Chuck is still working at the Club, the longest and maybe the oldest employee there. He had his retirement party some years back, but he keeps coming back to work.

Neville Wilson and Albert "Yokum" Edwards were in the next generation of caddies. Yokum remembers starting at $0.75 per round, while Neville remembers $1.00 per round. Tips varied from $0.25 to $1.00. Their pay was later raised to $1.25. Neville remembers going to Claude Rogers's store to buy a Coke and Moon Pie, both one nickel each. Back then, the caddy master was Harold Speed. There were fights between Franklin boys and Highlands boys. Several of the men I spoke to remember bullies, both from Franklin and Highlands. One of the favorite tricks was to grab a younger boy and put his head under the water of the pond that the caddies had dammed up. The consequences seemed to be in favor of the victims, who usually grabbed a rock and decked the bully. One Franklin boy was fired for bullying the others. Neville remembers walking from the Clear Creek area near what is now Queen Mountain to town and then to the Club. He caddied one whole month for a pro-golfer who played alone. Yokum remembers caddying for a group from Chattanooga and for George Woodruff. Then there was a cattleman by the name of Fred Hooper who played at the club. I believe he was from Alabama. He left Highlands when he bought a thoroughbred horse that he named Hoop Jr. His horse won the Kentucky Derby in 1945 with Eddie Arcaro as jockey. One of the other caddies went to Kentucky with Hooper to work for him. Yokum and his brother Dick walked from Horse Cove to the Club. Dick later moved to Alabama to raise horses and became a cowboy poet.

Yokum tells the story of one rainy day when he was caddying for George Woodruff. They were all sitting under the caddy shed waiting for the rain to stop. Mr. Woodruff told of a time that he was turkey hunting with Ty Cobb and Edgar Bergen. Mr. Woodruff and Edgar Bergen both shot at the same turkey, and both claimed that their shot brought it down. Edgar Bergen picked up the turkey and asked, "Who shot you?"

The turkey replied, "Bergen did, Bergen did."

Another incident that Yokum remembers was when Charlie Gibson's brother Clyde wanted to be a caddy. Now Clyde was on the short side, and the first time he picked up a golfer's bag, he dragged it on the ground because the bag was longer than Clyde. Harold Speed, the caddy master, caught up with him and sent him to the practice range, which at that time was the ninth fairway, to shag balls.

Coleman Reese's book *Life & Times of a Mountaineer* can be found at the Hudson Library, and it has a number of caddy stories. There were many other caddies from Highlands back in those days—Dugan Reese; Ray Reese; Leslie Reese, Bill Calloway and his brothers Jack, Scott and W.C.; Pearly Munger; and the Baty brothers, Earl, Buzz and Doc. According to Chuck

Crane, the era of the caddy came to an end in the 1950s. This was probably due to the advent of the golf cart, the increased number of players on the course and the need to speed up the game. At some point in the early days, caddies were issued badges. They were imprinted with HIGHLANDS COUNTRY CLUB CADDY (with a number) and their rank: A, B or C—A being the best.

If you ever want to see how the game would have been played back at the beginning, with or without a caddy, try the beaches on the east coast of the Isle of Lewis or the nine-hole course on the west coast of Iona, some of the Western Isles of Scotland. They make the Olde Course at St. Andrews look like the Augusta National. Just remember, there's no golf on Sunday on Lewis, but the rest of the week it's free.

MEMORIES OF HIGHLANDS INN: THE OLD DAYS

Well, sort of the old days. Let's say the late 1930s to the mid-1940s.

When I grew up, there was only one paved road into town. That was US 64 from Franklin to Cashiers. They paved Main Street about 1930—before my time. Imagine Main Street from the traffic light at the corner of Main and Fourth Streets, looking east toward the Presbyterian and Episcopal churches. The street was dirt and gravel, and there was an old tree in the middle of Main Street just off Fourth. Circling the tree was an island approximately twelve feet in diameter with a rock wall about three feet high. At one time it had a plaque on it noting the average elevation inside the city limits of the town at the time: 4,118 feet. It was called the "altitude oak," "charter oak" or just the "big oak."

On the right side of Main were the Central House and the recently built brick Hotel Edwards, the only one in town with steam heat. On the left side of the street was the rambling two- to three-story Highlands Inn. Both the Central House and Highlands Inn had a first- and second-floor porch, but the inn's first-floor porch was raised above street level.

Back then there were two lanes on Main Street with parking in the middle. Highlands Inn had a porch that was about three feet off the eastbound lane of the street. There was a railing on the porch just like the one now on the second floor and a laurel and rhododendron hedge between the first-floor railing and the street. On the west end of the porch, at the corner of Fourth and Main Streets, you walked up two steps to the beginning of the porch. This was Frank Cook's real estate and insurance office. It is a shop now. After

Highlands Inn, with Altitude Oak on the left.

that you went up two more steps to the main porch. Just past these steps was a door on the left leading to a dark, unfinished hall. There were steps from there to a nicely furnished apartment. It had a living room, kitchen, two bedrooms and a bath. This is where Frank and Verna Cook, owners of the inn, lived in the winter with their two daughters, Mary Bascom and Beverly. In the summer, they moved out and the apartment became guest rooms. At the east end of the porch where it ended was Talley and Burnette's store. Now it's Paoletti's Restaurant.

Mary Bascom, the older daughter, was my best friend. Her room moved so much that I never knew where to find her. One time when the inn was very full, I looked all over before finding five cots in the card room off the lobby. The family was all sleeping in there to make room for the paying guests. We had a very short season back then that ended on Labor Day. Everyone had to make it for the year between June and September.

The guests usually would come and stay from one month to three months, and they all seemed to enjoy the hospitality and the food. The dining room was open to non-guests on Sunday after church, and the food was very good.

There were more rocking chairs back then because it was a true porch. At the east end, it wrapped around the side of the inn all the way to the back. There were steps that went up to the third floor at that end to an enclosed sunroom with windows on three sides.

There was no access to the sidewalk at the east end, as there was no sidewalk to connect to. But as the town grew and more buildings were built east of the inn, the town board decided that it wasn't safe for pedestrians to walk out in the street around the porch of the inn. Because the street right of way actually came to the foundation of the inn, the porch had to be taken off, the laurel and rhododendron hedge removed and all lowered to street level. This created a mess, and getting into the inn became a real problem. It was solved by lowering the doorway going into the inn lobby and building steps inside to get back up to the original porch level. The doorway to Frank Cook's office was similarly lowered.

Everyone was upset to have this happen to our beautiful inn. As a compromise the town board allowed the inn to keep the rockers and flowers on what was the old porch.

We played hopscotch, May I, red rover and ping pong at the east end of the porch. In the winter, we played hide-and-seek all over the inn. I do miss my best friend and the porches. The "altitude oak" is gone along with the island surrounding it. I wish all of you could see it the way I remember it.

On August 13, 2005, the inn celebrated its 125th anniversary of being a part of Highlands.

THE BIG LAKE

Lake Sequoyah, Highlands' largest lake, is the first landmark one sees when approaching the Highlands Plateau on U.S. 64 coming from Franklin. It was constructed as a hydroelectric power lake for the town back in 1925–27 and went online in 1927 to supply electricity to the town. However, some areas continued to use their own sources of electricity, such as windmills that charged Delco batteries like the ones Dr. Anderson used at his house on Fifth Street. John Kaufman used water power from Big Creek to generate electric power in the late 1930s for his home on Buck Creek Road, even though Nantahala Power had its lines out there. Not all Highlanders used the new lighting source. Many continued to rely on oil lamps and wood stoves.

Lake Sequoyah.

There is a story that before the new power plant went into operation, some young boys thought it would be an adventure to slide down the steel flume line. After giving the idea some more thought, they went to the powerhouse and found that the line was capped off. Needless to say they were relieved that they hadn't tried the slide.

The lake became an immediate source of activity both in summer and winter. Lots were sold and homes built on the highway side of the lake. There was no road as yet on the far side of the lake. In the summer, townspeople and visitors would come to swim and boat. Tony experienced his first swimming lesson at the lake. In the winter, there was ice skating day and night. The lake was also the source for ice, which was cut out in blocks and hauled to commercial and private icehouses. When the ice was very thick, it was not unusual for cars to drive out on the ice during long cold winters. People of all ages would gather around the edge to sit by fires or skate.

One story has been told by a Charlestonian, Henry Ravenel, who participated in a lark during World War II. He and several other Clemson students flew up from South Carolina in the winter in a small plane, landed on the ice and hitched a ride into town to visit some young ladies.

The Roberts family built the first house, called Big Waters, on the back side of the lake. The builder was Joe Webb, well known in the area for his log cabins. The logs were floated across the lake, and the rest of the materials were rafted over. The log cabin still stands, and although a fire destroyed half the structure, it was restored by Tom Chambers, an antique log cabin restoration specialist.

Several creeks form the lake: Big Creek, Mill Creek and Munger Creek. In addition to these sources, there are several streams and the Cullasaja River that feed in from Mirror Lake.

There was a falls, called Kalakalaski Falls, that was covered when the lake was created. Before that, these falls were a favorite picnic destination that was closer than Bridal Veil Falls and Dry Falls, which were located farther down U.S. 64. The town commissioners selected the name for the lake from a number of suggestions. It is an anglicized version of "sikwa'ya," the name of a Cherokee chief, Sequoyah, also known as George Guess. He was the son of an itinerant white farmer, named Gist, and a half-Cherokee mother. You may recall this is the man that created the Cherokee alphabet.

The Cullasaja River flows into the lake over Naiad Falls. Cullasaja is another Cherokee name, which is thought to mean "sweet water" and was originally named Sugar Fork before taking a Cherokee name.

Some information was provided by Peggy Watkins' book *Webbmont* and Dr. Randolph Shaffner's book *Heart of the Blue Ridge*.

An Old-Time Christmas in Highlands

It was just after Thanksgiving when the youngest son of Tudor Tucker Hall and Meta Norton Frost Hall asked his father about going to get the Christmas tree.

"No Tudor, you know it's too early to get the tree. Why, by the time Christmas came there wouldn't be a needle left." Young Tudor Hall persisted. He had just turned six in September, and Christmas was a very important day, almost as important as his birthday. After a week passed with the question being asked several times a day, the sixty-seven-year-old veteran of the Civil War relented.

"Come on Tudor, go get your brother Jack; he'll have to do the chopping. Tell him to bring the sharpest axe." They went out to the carriage house and had one of the men that worked year-round at the Hall House hitch up one of the horses to the buggy.

Jack Hall was eleven and behaved like he was the man of the place. He ran out from the main house carrying the axe and jumped up on the seat alongside his younger brother and father. T.T. Hall made sure that Jack cut down several trees. They would put one up in the living room, use another to make wreaths for the front door and use two more for the graves of Mattie Norton, Meta's mother, and Dr. Frost, Meta's first husband. I guess little Tudor's insistence on getting the trees was a good idea after all. The following day it started snowing, and the woods where T.T. Hall usually found his trees were too deep in snow to get in. Christmas at the Hall House was a special occasion. The summer guests had been gone since September, and the family had moved back into the main house so the older children could have their own room.

Hall House, Christmas 1911.

In several other stories we have told you about T.T. Hall and Meta Norton Frost Hall and their large family—a family who ranged in age from one to thirteen plus T.T.'s family from his first marriage. Now Deas and Judge Broyles were coming up from Atlanta to spend the holidays, as well as Harry from the eastern part of North Carolina.

Well, the snow didn't slow down any of the preparations for Christmas. Meta had begun making candy and fruitcake right after Thanksgiving. Dorothy and Mattie, the oldest daughters, began stringing popcorn to decorate the tree. Jack and Mattie, with Dorothy's help and instructions from their mother, would go into the woods and pull up moss off of dead logs and then cut chicken wire to make the frames for the cemetery wreath. They would then stuff the moss inside the tubular frame and cut short pieces of pine and hemlock and stick them in the frame. The whole family rode over to the cemetery before Christmas and put the wreaths on Dr. Frost's grave. David Norton, Meta's father, would join them at the cemetery.

Little Tudor ran around, getting under everyone's feet, and baby Caroline didn't know what to make of all the commotion. Santa Clause had not yet become a roly-poly fat man in a red suit. He was depicted on cards and pictures as a rather slender gentleman dressed in a fur-trimmed knee-length coat of a royal crimson color and wore a fur-fringed cap. But to the children in the Hall House, it was a magical time and one to be remembered from year to year. The older ones would tell tall stories about St. Nicholas and tease their younger siblings about coal in their shoes instead of candy.

Finally, a few days before Christmas, Harry arrived in his new motorcar. He was unmarried and lived in the eastern part of the state. His visits were always a treat for his younger half brothers and sisters. As he had no children, he loved to bring them presents, whether or not it was Christmas. The next day, Deas and Judge Broyles arrived from Atlanta. It had been a hard trip for both. They would come up to Dillard on the Tallulah Falls Railroad and then get a horse-drawn hack and ride up the mountain. At least now there were cars, so the trip didn't take two days, as it did earlier in the century. Deas was somewhat younger than the judge. He was a friend of T.T. Hall. Now the festivities started. Since the dining room was quite large, the Halls had invited a number of their friends for dinner, including David Norton from town. There were numbered prints of various birds by Pope that hung on the walls. These had been prizes awarded to Mr. Hall when he lived in Charleston.

The younger children would eat early and would peek from the top of the stairs to see all the guests. Several times T.T. Hall would call up the stairs to send them back to their rooms, but they would only retreat out of sight until he returned to the dining room. Mrs. Hall did have help, although she oversaw the cooking herself. It was also a time she enjoyed. During the summer, she really had the management of the hotel all by herself since Mr. Hall was really getting too old to be active. Oh, he would charm the ladies and take the gentlemen hunting or skeet shooting. He had been a champion marksman in his prime. But the daily routine of seeing that the rooms were cleaned, beds made, laundry done and serving three meals a day was all she had time to do. So entertaining in the winter was enjoyable.

All the children's presents had been hidden away in empty, locked guest bedrooms. And the tree was sitting outside on the back porch to keep it from drying out. The day before Christmas, though, everyone gathered in the living room, and Mr. Hall's handyman brought in the tree with its homemade stand. Mattie and Dorothy fought to be the first to decorate the tree with the popcorn strings. Then Mrs. Hall brought out the boxes of German ornaments that Mr. Hall had brought when he came to Highlands. Finally, Jack clamped the small candleholders to the strongest branches. These would be lit Christmas morning when everyone came down to open the presents. No presents were brought in until all the children had gone to bed Christmas Eve.

Christmas morning was like everyone's home in the world. Children going into their parents' rooms begging them to get up. But Harry was already up. He had slipped out of bed and was dressed. He was the one who lit the candles and watched to make sure nothing caught on fire, and he lit the fire in the fireplace. The cook was not there until dinnertime later in the afternoon, so he went to the kitchen and started a fire in the wood stove so Meta could make coffee when she came down. Then, with a rush of feet, the children came down the stairs and gathered around the tree. They waited until T.T., Meta (carrying baby Caroline), Deas and the judge arrived. The adults then sat down as each of the children carefully took a package and opened it. There were squeals of joy from the girls and a shout from Jack as he opened the long, slim package and held out his first rifle. Little Tudor was at first troubled by the size of his box but then let out a whoop when he saw what was inside. It was a sailboat that his father had made. He had wished for a sailboat to float on their lake.

Harry then got down on his hands and knees and started handing presents to young and old alike. He had brought his sister Deas a new hat of the latest fashion and a smoking jacket for the judge. He hoped that it would be fitting

156

present for him. He gave his stepmother Meta a warm wool coat. He had noticed last Christmas that she usually just put on a wool shawl in the coldest weather. Her eyes gleamed as she leaned down and kissed him. Before all the presents had been opened, Mrs. Hall asked Mattie to look after baby Caroline, slipped out of the room and went to the kitchen. She mentally thanked her thoughtful stepson for starting the fire in the stove. He had even filled the coffee pot with water and set it on the back where it could be warming up. She quickly mixed up her biscuit dough and put them in the oven. In just a few minutes, she called Dorothy to set the table in the dining room. Then she called everyone into the dining room, where she had hot biscuits, sliced ham, scrambled eggs, jam, coffee and milk for the children. Mattie was the only youngster who reacted with the adults. She came in carrying Caroline and handed her to Meta. Jack and Tudor were too excited to think about eating.

By mid-afternoon, help had come in and finished up what was left to do in the kitchen and then served a large ham with sweet potatoes and all the trimmings. David had arrived before dinner, and T.T. and Meta had given her father a new winter coat. By then, the children were really hungry; they gobbled down their meal and asked to be excused to go outside and play in the snow.

Judge Broyles and Deas stayed two more days and then started on their journey back to Atlanta. They had social engagements that required them to leave earlier than usual. Harry stayed until after New Years. He sold life insurance and didn't feel that rushing home to an empty apartment during the holidays was the least bit interesting. He enjoyed his young half brothers and sisters and would have stayed longer if he didn't have to make a living.

This story is based on the recollections of Isabel's father, T.N. Hall, from that Christmas of 1911.

POUNDING, BACONING AND OTHER OLD SOCIAL CUSTOMS

A friend of ours suggested that we cover some old mountain social customs. The first one that came to mind was the custom of pounding. It could be related to the more familiar term: house warming. We don't know where the practice originated, but here in the mountains it was a way of getting newlyweds set up in housekeeping or families moved into their first home. The name literally means bringing a pound of something that a family might need: salt, flour, sugar, coffee and more. Just last year, the Episcopal church had a pounding for our new minister, Brian Sullivan, and his wife Mindy.

Some other types of gatherings for welcoming newlyweds or those moving into a home were called shivaree or serenading. Isabel and I were serenaded when we moved into our first house in Highlands. Usually it is a surprise, but not always. In our case, it was a surprise. The custom includes singing (of a sort) and loud music, and tradition has it that the couple heated pennies in an iron skillet and then tossed them to the crowd outside. Needless to say, this practice must have dated back to far earlier times, when a penny was worth something. In our case, several of the other traditions were still in practice: riding the wife around in a wheelbarrow and the husband on a rail. We did appreciate the food that everyone brought. We remember some of the couples involved back then: Bob and Jean Rice; our United States Forest Service ranger John Connell and his wife Varina; Earl and Mary Lou Young; and Isabel's parents, Margaret and Tudor Hall. Sadly, all of them are gone except Earl. I guess we were the youngest.

Some twenty years earlier, Margaret and Tudor, and Docky and Bessie (Isabel's parents and grandparents), had a planned pounding-housewarming. They had just finished building their home on Fifth Street in 1933. Besides food and gifts, they had a dance on their new oak hardwood floors. There wasn't much furniture at that point, so there was plenty of room to dance. It was one of those gatherings that doesn't occur very often nowadays. Summer residents and locals joined in to welcome their local dentist and master plumber and electrician in their new home. Highlands Country Club was just a few years old at the time, but many of the new summer people, including Bobby Jones, came to welcome the two families and dance. Isabel doesn't remember much about the party but remembers her parents and grandparents talking about it.

Another old custom, baconing, has apparently died out. Couples would get together and take ham, eggs and grits, probably, and hike up Sunset Rock to have breakfast at sunset. I heard Tudor say that hardier souls would get up early and do the same thing on Sunrise Rock. Get-togethers like baconing were pretty popular back sixty or seventy years ago or more. Most of the time they included a hike. Another social event was held in Horse Cove, at the Hill House, we believe. The bachelors would hike down from Highlands, and perhaps from Whiteside Cove and Horse Cove, in the early evening and

Tennis court at the Hutchinson-Frost-Hall-Farnsworth Home with Deas Hall Broyles in the foreground, circa 1910.

meet at the Hill House for a dance. I think they called it "sparking" back then. Tudor never said what else happened, only that the young ladies would heat potatoes in the cookstove and give them to the men to keep their hands warm on the way home.

Have we left out sports gatherings? No, they're next. Isabel had a tennis court in her backyard when she was growing up, the last vestige of the Hall House sports program. The children would run after the balls that went over the fence or to the side in the woods. After the adults tired, they would usually cut a watermelon. Across the street, Dr. Alexander P. Anderson and his wife Lydia had a court. The Hutchinson-Frost-Hall-Farnsworth Home had a tennis court, as well as the Kelsey Home across the street. The Northrups had a court at their home on Hickory Street, once owned by Isabel's aunt and uncle, Dorothy and Roy Potts, and most recently sold by Ran and Margaret Shaffner to Karen and Terry Potts. There was one court at the Rabbit Hole on Spring Street, one at the Terhune place out off Dillard Road and another out at the Morrison place near the Highlands-Cashiers Hospital campus.

The town's first tennis court was located up on School House Hill, where the ABC store is now. It was a clay court, located on the site of the old school outdoor basketball court. It would wash after every rain. "Snook" Thompson, Tony, Reverend Robert B. DuPree and other recreation park directors had more trouble with that court than all of the rest of their jobs put together. But the private courts were the gathering spots for the folks that didn't play golf, and there were a lot of them. Many times the owners' friends would bring picnics to enjoy after a round of singles and doubles.

Before the Nantahala Hiking Club, the young people in Highlands went on a lot of picnics. They would walk or ride horses from the livery stables to Whiteside Mountain by way of the Kelsey Trail, up to the summit of Satulah or down to Dry Falls before the Franklin Road was built.

Churches had more daytime gatherings back then. Many of them were fundraisers. The Episcopal church had Silver Teas. Each year, someone volunteered their home, and the women of the church would prepare light food, tea and punch—soft of course. The name "silver" had a double meaning. The hosts would bring out their finest silver tea service, and the guests were expected to bring the other kind of silver, back when coins were made with that metal. Back in the 1910s and '20s, the women of the Episcopal church usually raised the money to pay the priests that were invited to come and give services in the summer. The Silver Teas brought in most of the cash for this. Other churches had musicals featuring local pianists and singers.

Of course we couldn't tell you about the old-time social events and leave out Helen's Barn. Much has been written about the barn, how it came to be and what happened to it. But the fact that we had a place to dance for such a long time, from the early 1930s to the early 1980s, is a testament to its popularity; it was a great equalizer of the summer residents and the locals. Your authors danced there in the 1940s and again in the early '70s when they returned to stay. When the string band took a break between sets, the jukebox was there for those that still had strength. The selections ranged from jitterbug to fox trot to waltzes. We can remember Tony's mother, Day Way, and Admiral Newton McCully dancing to a classic waltz or a lively polka, whirling around the floor, and Callie Beal doing her thing—buck dancing. It is a great tribute to Helen Wilson and later the Wright family to continue Helen's Barn for such a long stand.

So if you hear someone ask, "What's there to do in Highlands?" tell them what the earlier residents did to amuse themselves.

PART IV

FAMILY

MY SISTER SARAH

Sarah has been featured in several of our stories. She was my older and only sister. From the stories, you can tell she was brave, adventuresome, outgoing and lovable.

Now I'll tell you about the real Sarah. She wasn't afraid of anything and I was—timid, shy, afraid, that was me. She loved to fish. I didn't like it. We lived near Mill Creek, and to get to the side of the creek you had to walk through high grass, which I knew hid snakes and bugs and critters. Back then we didn't wear blue jeans. We were proper little girls and wore short dresses. So when she wanted to go down to the creek and fish, she would promise to walk in first and tramp down the grass and bait my hook, and if I caught anything she would take the fish off the hook. All I had to do was hold my pole. That was boring.

Then there was the time she decided to find out if our cat had nine lives. One afternoon she got a feed sack out of the shop, put in some rocks and had me hold it open while she caught the cat and put it in the sack. Then we slipped out of the house and went down to the creek. She tied the sack with a piece of twine so it couldn't get out, and so the cat was hissing and snarling like all get out. When we got to the creek, she put the sack in the water, but it wasn't under the water completely. We started back home, and she decided that the cat probably had enough. When she pulled the sack out of the water, the cat was still hissing and snarling to beat the band, so she untied the twine and the cat jumped out and headed for home.

Well, that was one life, and the cat had eight to go. Several days later, Dama went into the kitchen to start breakfast. She heard something out on the porch and went to see what the noise was. It was coming from the new electric stove that Daddy had installed (he had just started selling them). We had a perfectly good wood stove in the kitchen, and Dama liked it. She didn't think the electric stove would get hot enough. She opened it and almost fell down when the cat jumped out and ran out. Mother heard the racket and came to see what had happened. Then she called Sarah. I don't know how she knew, but mothers have that sixth sense. Naturally, Sarah was very proud that the cat hadn't died with her experiment. Mother didn't quite see it that way. When we got home from school that afternoon, the cat was gone and never came back.

Then there was the time in Florida when Sarah decided that she was going to capture an animal. You've heard of palmetto bugs. Well, they scare me to death, they're so big. Now Sarah has no fear of man, beast or palmetto bugs. One afternoon, when we were outside on the porch, she caught one and slipped a piece of thread over one leg. She then held the other end of the thread while the bug flew around in circles. When we were called to supper, she tied her end of the thread onto a chair. We forgot about it after dinner, but when we went outside the next morning to check to see if the bug was still there we had a surprise. At the bug end of the thread was a dead frog lying on its back with the thread coming out of his mouth.

Did I mention salamanders? Well, Sarah practiced being a doctor at home, too. Back then salamanders, black ones and orange ones, were common around our block. One spring day, she caught one and decided that she would practice setting a broken leg. Of course, the salamander didn't have a broken leg, but that was all right. She got mother's fingernail polish remover out and put some on a rag and chloroformed the salamander. Then she got a matchstick and thread and set one of the salamander's legs. Then she filled a bucket part way with water and put a rock in it, so the salamander could be in water and get on the rock if it wanted to. She left the bucket outside, and the next morning when she checked the salamander in the bucket, the water had frozen and the salamander was frozen, too. She felt sorry for the critter and put the chunk of ice under hot water. When the ice melted, the salamander wriggled around some, and so Sarah took the splint off its leg and let it go. No, she did not grow up to be a doctor.

Family

My Brother Buddy

I've written a lot about my older sister Sarah and the adventures she led me on, but this is my brother Buddy's story. I have two brothers: Tudor G. "Buddy" and John T. Hall. Buddy is no longer with us. I have lots of memories of him, mostly ones of his early years. He took after my dad a lot—inquisitive, inventive and always getting his friends to go along with whatever he wanted to do. He was eighteen months younger than I, and as I was in the middle, I tried to please both Sarah and Bud. Sarah and I called him "Brudder" since we couldn't pronounce "brother." That evolved into Buddy. Sarah would never play dolls with me, nor would Bud, so we played train. He got a wonderful Lionel freight train that puffed smoke and made a real steam whistle sound. A year later he got an American Flyer stream liner train with a sleek, modern, green and yellow engine and passenger cars to match. The last car was an observation car with a modern rounded-off end. All of the cars had lights in their windows. The year he got the passenger train, I got a big colonial-style dollhouse, just like our home.

We had a whole room designated for my dollhouse and his railroad track. When my brother Johnny was born, this became his room. There were switches that took the train all around the room to an erector set, where we set up a sawmill and loaded and unloaded Lincoln logs off the train's flatcar. There was a siding that took the passenger train to the resort hotel, my dollhouse. We would play at night with the room lights turned off. Then we watched in the dark as the trains went around the tracks with their lights on and with the lights that my dad had put in the dollhouse. Every ten times around the tracks, Bud would blow the old freight train whistle and then the modern passenger train horn. When a train went off the track, I put it back on. When I would turn the switch to send the passenger train to the siding to the hotel, I'd better get it right or the train would jump the track and wreck—and it was my job to fix it. Bud controlled everything else. That was our winter indoor fun.

When summer came, we played cars on a dirt bank with tree roots as obstacles for our roads to go around. We had all the scenic places we have here today, and our roads were just as bad and curvy. Later, we used old lumber from a pile left over when our house was built to make or build cars, boats, airplanes and castles in the backyard. The castle was a playhouse with two floors; that's why we called it a castle. It had real stairs that went up to the roof so we could look down on our subjects. When Buddy was

Left to right, front seat: David Brown and Buddy Hall. *Back seat*: Charles Major.

older, Daddy gave him new lumber, nails and a hammer. Then he built a real playhouse with floors, doors and windows. By this time I could nail almost as good as Buddy, so I was his carpenter's helper. But I couldn't saw, so I got Sarge Gibson to cut boards the length I needed. I believe I could build a house today if I had to. As we got older, I lost him to his friends: boys and girls. But I was his chauffer when he started having girlfriends and couldn't drive.

When Buddy was in his early, early teens, he was given an eight-millimeter movie camera. I'll bet his movies would have made a splash at the Sundance Film Festival. His best friends were Joe and Charles Major, who lived across the street at the Sullivan house in the summer. Buddy decided to make a movie about moonshiners. It was called *Pass That Jug*. All three of them dressed up in the dirtiest clothes, blackened their teeth and went up on Sunset. They looked like something out of *Li'l Abner*. They shot part of the movie there and the rest in our backyard. One of the scenes on Sunset was of Charles walking on the trail that turned off to the right before you get to

164

the cliff. Buddy liked to use black powder made by the DuPont Chemical Company. He poured some on the trail and then started shooting Charles walking down the trail. He stopped the camera when Charles was at the spot where the black powder was poured. Then he told Charles to spit and get out of the scene. Buddy then lit a fuse to the black powder and started the camera again pointed at the spot where Charles had been standing. He got a shot of the puff of smoke. When the film was developed, it looked just like Charles's spit had exploded. Another shot was of a dummy with similar clothes being thrown over the cliff. Back in our yard, he had the actors sitting around a still with a fire going. He painted three Coca-Cola gallon syrup bottles brown to look like clay jugs, painted the word "Pass" on one jug, "That" on the next jug and "Jug" on the third. He hung them from a tree on long ropes above the actors. He panned from the actors to close in on the jugs, and then he stopped the camera. He got the actors away from the jugs, and one of them shot the jugs with his .22 rifle. That was the title scene of the movie.

Another movie was made across the street at the Sullivan house. This was a haunted house movie, with Joe as a demented butler and so on. He shot it in the early evening. It came out just like the horror movies: dark and you could barely see the characters.

As I remember, Buddy was a tinkerer. He bought an oscilloscope from Heathkit and put it together. Another time he built some kind of electric gadget. It had two poles, and when he turned it on, electricity arced between the poles. It was low voltage, so you could put your hand between the poles.

When Buddy was in his mid-teens, Tony's father asked Buddy and Tony to fix up an old toolshed into a sort of guesthouse with a bathroom. The first job was to replace a rotten sill on the downhill side. I think Tony's father thought that Buddy knew a lot because of my father always having him help. Anyway, they got building jacks and started raising the small structure to get at the rotten sill. It wasn't until the building started swaying that they realized they didn't need to raise all four sides. They lowered the building and finished the job without telling anyone. Then they started on the inside. Mr. Chambers wanted a shower in the bathroom and bought a metal one along with the lavatory. They finished installing all the plumbing and connected the water. When one of them turned on the shower, it sprayed right out of the shower curtain section. So they took it apart and moved the opening away from the showerhead.

When he was about twenty, he and Tony found an old Model T. It took a while to get a title for it, but Buddy started working on it and got it running.

It didn't have a body—just a windshield, front and rear fenders and hood. That was the first year we had Hillbilly Day. The tires were rotten, so he tied rags around the wood wheels between the spokes to keep the tires on. Everyone dressed up to look like a hillbillies, including Charles, Tony, Joe and Buddy, maybe "Snook" Thompson. Anyway, we had a parade, and the Model T ran through most of it. Each year after that, the Model T took on a different life. One year it had a black tin body, and my sister Sarah and I rode in it with our sons Scott and Tucker in baby clothes, with my father driving and mother next to him in the front seat. Another year it served Dr. Fudd's Medicine Show with a plywood body painted black to look like an old-time medicine wagon. Another year it was converted into a flying saucer from outer space. Buddy finally sold the old car, and Wilbur Simmons took it to Florida and restored it beautifully. Those are my memories of Buddy.

FAREWELL TO A QUEEN

We are referring to someone who has appeared in several of our history articles over the past years, but she was never the main character. We would like to tell you about this woman, my mother, who has touched so many lives in Highlands.

Margaret, Marg, Mother, Mema—she was born in Atlanta, Georgia, while her father was attending Atlanta Dental College. Since then she lived in Kansas City, Kansas; Salt Lake City, Utah; Sage, Wyoming; Nebo, North Carolina; and Westminster, South Carolina. She finally came to Highlands for several summers in the early 1920s with her parents, Bessie and Elbert Gilbert. Her father was practicing dentistry in Westminster at the time and later would set up his practice in the Central House, High Hampton Inn or wherever they were staying. But that first summer, 1922, the family camped beside Mirror Lake. After several summers camping, Miss Margaret Harry, a Delano nurse, asked Dr. Gilbert if he would set a summer practice in Highlands. So in the summer of 1924 they moved to Highlands and Margaret attended Highlands School.

She would relate that she first noticed Tudor Norton Hall, her future husband, when he drove a stripped-down car of unknown origin down Main Street in front of the Central House with a monkey called "Old Folks" on his back. When she inquired as to whom the young man was, she learned that he was the son of a wealthy heiress, Meta Norton Frost Hall. After moving

Margaret Gilbert Hall.

to Highlands, she apparently set her cap for Tudor, as they were married in 1928 after she graduated from high school.

Tudor was a member of the Episcopal Church of the Incarnation, as were his mother and Norton grandparents, but it was closed at the time of their wedding. Margaret and her parents had been attending the Presbyterian church. So a compromise was reached, and the Presbyterian minister conducted the ceremony at Incarnation. A few years later, Incarnation secured a full-time priest, Reverend Norvin Duncan, and the Gilbert family joined Incarnation along with Margaret.

Their first child, Sarah, was born in 1930. I was born one year later, and our younger brother, Tudor G. "Buddy," was born in 1932. Mother and Grandmother Gilbert taught Sunday school in those early days. Mother would drive to outlying areas to pick up the Keener and Zachary children, as well as others, and bring them to Sunday school. Mattie Zachary Crawford recalled those Sundays recently. I asked if she remembered just how everyone fit in the car but she didn't remember and I don't either. Mother also designed our first rectory, which was built in the mid-1930s. It was located where Mountain Findings was located and is now the site of the new Highlands Community Child Development Center. Margaret and Tudor, as well as Bessie Gilbert, were dependable volunteers at Incarnation.

She served as secretary, treasurer and president of the Episcopal Church Women at Incarnation, as well as on the Altar Guild. Before that time, only spinsters were on the Altar Guild. Later, as her children grew older, she became active in diocesan events, such as Michaelmas, a medieval pageant and a fair.

She and Tudor bought the real estate and insurance agency of S.T. Marett back in the early 1940s when Tudor hurt his back and could no longer run his electrical and plumbing business. This was shortly after John Tucker was born, the youngest of their four children. They were the first Realtors® in Highlands. In fact, they joined the National Association of Real Estate Agents years before North Carolina started licensing real estate agents.

Back in the '40s, Mother and my grandmother, Dama, were members of a bridge club. And they took it very seriously. Other members were Martha Cobb, Verna Cook, Sara Gilder, Helen "Madam Queen" Potts, Lydia "Bites" Harcombe and Helen Story. If you knew Highlands back then, you'd know what kind of group that was. We hated it when Mother and Grandmother had the club. The house had to be cleaned—I mean really cleaned. One time my youngest brother John decided he would play a trick on the ladies. They always had coffee or tea, so he emptied the sugar bowl and filled it with salt. Did he catch it! Mother enjoyed bridge, but when our grandmother died, she quit playing. She picked it up again when another club called the Stewed Tomatoes asked her to play, and she was a welcome substitute with that group.

In the 1950s, she discovered she could dowse for water. Henry Gross, a retired Maine game warden, came to Highlands to dowse a well for the town. Gross was a friend of Kenneth Roberts, author of *Northwest Passage* and other historical novels. The two men had formed a corporation, Water Unlimited, Inc., and Gross traveled all over the country dowsing wells. So Margaret became a water witch and was in great demand from well drillers. She dowsed many producing wells and continued to perform this service into her eighties. She even received Christmas presents from well drillers like Bruce Hedden. Though she didn't take money for dowsing, she asked that the property owners make a donation to Incarnation.

In the 1950s, she and Tudor took time on weekends to look for semiprecious stones. They formed a Rock Hound Club and found old mines in the area. When they found an interesting garnet or amethyst, mother would take it to Archie Jellen to be cut and mounted into a piece of jewelry. Since they didn't keep their real estate and insurance office open on weekends, my brother and sister would pester them to go camping. We promised to set up the tent, usually in Horse Cove or down Satulah Falls Lane, buy the food and have everything ready when they closed the office Friday afternoon. Usually, we would each bring a friend or two so it got to be a big affair. You might say it was a great way to bring a boy or girl friend for an overnight and have happy chaperones.

In the 1950s and '60s, Tony and I got into folk music. I had been teaching piano and then started teaching baritone ukulele and guitar. Mother decided she wanted to learn, so on weekends when we were in Highlands, I started her on the baritone ukulele, but she went on to the guitar and dulcimer. Well, from playing "On Top of Old Smoky" and "Tom Dooley," she went on to write her own lyrics to old ballads. I learned that my mother would try anything.

Mother started the home tours, along with Father Gale Webbe, to raise money for the church. (Back then there wasn't much to do around town.) She chaired and helped with many Silver Teas. She served a term on our vestry, served on several Future Planning Committees for the church and was on the Centennial History Book task force. She could also tell you just about everything that was done at the church from 1928 to the early 1980s.

She got my dad interested in traveling—I mean across the big water. They joined a travel club and usually went somewhere every year. Their first trip was to Bermuda. Mother had started getting interested in genealogy and hoped to find information about Tudor's grandfather, Henry Tucker Hall, who was born in Bermuda.

On one trip, a Mediterranean cruise, they stopped in Egypt. There was a side trip to the see the pyramids at Giza. They took a train and finally a bus to get to Giza. Their guide instructed them not to get off the bus when they arrived because of the lack of security. Untrustworthy camel drivers! But mother said she didn't come all that way to see the pyramids from the window of a bus. Out she went and Tudor followed. Almost immediately a camel driver had her up in the saddle and started off with her. The guide rushed up and had a quick conversation with the camel driver. Tudor asked what was happening. The guide said the camel driver wanted so much money to bring Margaret back. I wasn't there, but I always wondered if my father hesitated a while before paying up.

On another trip, to Central America, they were in San Salvador, and at the time there were rebels fighting the government. As they were touring downtown San Salvador on a bus, there were sounds of gunfire. The driver stopped and everyone got out except Margaret and Tudor. My father told Marg that if she wasn't going to get out of the bus, she should at least get down on the floor. She replied that she wasn't going to get down on that dirty floor. And she wasn't scared. They were seated near the rear of the bus, and she had Tudor's camera in her hand. When they got home and developed the film, there were half dozen shots of the rearview mirror at the front of the bus with the image in the mirror of them seated in the rear. My mother didn't like to be told what to do.

My father died in 1985, and we didn't know how mother would handle it. She needed something to do. I suggested she start a bed-and-breakfast, but there was no ordinance to allow this. Mother, Mary Bascom Cook and I requested a new town law to allow the business ventures. Mary B. wanted to turn her home next to the ballpark into a B & B also. By June of that same year, we got the new ordinance, and mother opened up the Hall House, with four bedrooms upstairs. There was a little remodeling to be done: adding another bathroom upstairs, moving mother downstairs, setting up an office and getting trays and so forth with which to serve breakfast in the rooms. She worried about people wanting to lock their rooms, so we scoured the town for skeleton keys that would fit the old door locks on the upstairs bedrooms. She was very selective in her guests. Usually she only took reservations in advance, but occasionally she would take walk-ins. On one occasion, a young couple asked for a room, and she asked if they were married. They didn't answer, but mother decided not to take them. Mother kept the "Hall House" open for about five years but finally decided that she had had enough company.

When we moved our office to mother's home in 1993, we built an apartment on the back of the house. Mother was ready to take a less active role in the housekeeping and the community. She had contributed much to Highlands, and it was time to take a rest. With twelve grandchildren, twenty-five great-grandchildren and three great-great-grandchildren, she had done her part. She reigned as queen on her scarlet throne with over one hundred well-wishers on her ninetieth birthday at the High Country Café restaurant just four years ago.

Mother died on Friday, May 13, at the Fidelia Eckard Living Center after a short illness.

Had this not happened, she might have taken over the place. When she checked in, I told everyone that she was "the Queen." They quickly told me that they had several already. Although she was very weak and had difficulty walking when she moved in, by the next week she was strolling along in her walker to the dining room and chatting up everyone on her way back.

She was not a native but lived here long enough to claim that title.

TUDOR NORTON HALL

We've often included genealogical history in our articles. Perhaps at our age, we look back on those that came before us and try to imagine what life was like for our grandparents and great-grandparents. Tony often says that people in the South seem to have a greater extended family than those that grew up in the North or Midwest. Take my father, for example. He grew up not ten miles from where Barak Norton, his twice great-grandfather on his mother's side, lived in Whiteside Cove almost two hundred years ago. I have second and third Norton cousins I've never met who live here in Western North Carolina. So I would like to tell you about my father, Tudor Norton Hall.

Pepa, as his grandchildren called him, was born in Highlands in September 1905. He was the second son and fourth child of Meta Norton Frost Hall's five children. His mother was previously married to Dr. Charles Frost but had no children by that marriage. Dr. Frost had encouraged Tudor Tucker Hall and his wife, Harriet, to move to Highlands from their home in Charleston, South Carolina. It was 1889, and Dr. Frost had built a new house for Meta on the back of his property and was ready to sell the house that he bought from Clinton C. Hutchinson, co-founder of Highlands. T.T. Hall had been looking for a more agreeable climate for Harriet, his ten-year-old daughter Deas and his eight year-old-son Harry. Highlands looked to be the right place. The Halls and the Frosts became good friends and shared one another's table on many occasions. Both couples—along with Meta's father, David Norton; Dr. Henry T. O'Farrell; and Jeremiah Pierson—were the core of the Episcopal congregation in Highlands. Their priest was Reverend Archibald Deal, who had been a circuit rider in Western North Carolina since 1879. He founded St. John's, the first Episcopal church in Macon County at Cartoogechaye near Franklin.

Tragically, Dr. Frost and Harriet Hall died in 1893. This left Meta and T.T. without spouses and, more importantly, his two children without a mother. However, Deas, his oldest child, married a close friend of his, Judge Nash Broyles, in 1894. After Dr. Frost's death, Meta started helping her father

Tudor Norton Hall.

David at the Central House. But romance blossomed, and in March 1896 Meta and T.T. were married in the Central House, with Reverend Deal officiating. It is said that she carved their initials in the window glass on the Main Street side of the hotel next to the old fireplace with her diamond wedding ring. The new Episcopal church, Incarnation, was completed in the fall of the same year. The Meadow House, as Dr. Frost and Meta named the new home near Chestnut Street, was a larger house, and the newlyweds decided to sell the Hutchinson-Frost-Hall home on Horse Cove Road to Patrick Farnsworth from Memphis, Tennessee.

It didn't take long for the couple to start a family: Mattie arrived in 1898, Jack in 1900, Dorothy in 1902, my dad in 1905 and Caroline in 1910. Shortly after their marriage, T.T. and Meta began to create a summer resort on their property. The house was added on to and a lake was created— later a nine-hole golf course, a dance pavilion and a clay tennis court were added. T.T. had been a sportsman in Charleston: champion trap shooter, bird hunter and golfer. Theirs was just one of many tennis courts in town. As the children grew, they were pressed into helping at the resort, now being called the Hall House. Friends from Charleston; Aiken, South Carolina; and

Atlanta became their first guests. As the two boys grew older, Jack and my dad would drive the car that their father bought but didn't know how to drive. Imagine the shock when a ten- or twelve-year-old boy would meet hotel guests at the train in Dillard or Seneca. Many guests would spend the entire summer.

T.T. died in 1918 when my dad was thirteen. Meta had always employed women from around Highlands to help, but with the management of the resort solely on her shoulders, the children were pressed into service more and more. My dad was already mowing the lawn, keeping the golf course up and managing the vegetable garden. But Meta thought that he needed more schooling and enrolled him in Rabun-Gap Nacoochee, a boarding school near Dillard, Georgia. My dad wasn't about to become a farmer after his work in the hotel garden, so he didn't stay at Rabun Gap-Nacoochee School. Jack was sent to Clemson, and Daddy was a little turned off by his mother's educational plans for him. I think he was close to sixteen when he got a job in Atlanta with the telephone company. Later he went to Jacksonville, Florida, to work for a telephone company there. That experience came in good stead when Meta leased the telephone company in Highlands. Daddy moved back to Highlands, and he and Jack strung wires, installed phones and repaired lines, while some of their sisters manned the switchboard.

Daddy went on to learn about electricity and was hired by the Town of Highlands to manage the new generating plant at Lake Sequoyah. This led to working for the new Nantahala Power Company, and from that he branched out on his own to be an electrical and plumbing contractor. This included everything from selling kitchen appliances to installing septic systems. Before this period of transition, my mother had moved to Highlands with her parents, Dr. E.R. Gilbert and Bessie Isabel Hall Gilbert (no relation to Daddy). Dr. Gilbert became the town dentist. Mother had fallen for Daddy when she first saw him driving in a stripped-down roadster on Main Street. She was apparently mature for her age, as she was just sixteen and had graduated from high school when they married. They didn't have any money, and there wasn't any room at the Hall House, since his sister Dorothy had married Roy Potts and they were living there with their two-year-old daughter, as well as Roy's sister Caroline, his brother Jack and his mother.

So, Daddy and Mother moved in with Docky (Elbert) and Bessie. It's not any easier today, is it? Along with all the other jobs that Daddy held, he helped Docky when he leased the Highlands Hardware Store. Meta started transferring her property to the children in the early 1930s. Docky and my dad decided to build a house on some of Daddy's property. It was 1933, and there was no chance of getting a bank mortgage; both my dad and Docky bartered for everything to build the house, including labor and materials. They finished the first floor and left the second floor unfinished. There were four rooms—the kitchen, the living-dining room, two bedrooms—and one bathroom. My folks shared their bedroom with myself, my sister Sarah and my brother Buddy—three cribs and a double bed. When we got a little older, the second floor was finished with four bedrooms and another bath.

Since the church was very important in their lives, and the congregation was not large, Daddy became janitor, repairman and vestryman. Since we lived just a block away, Daddy would see to it that on cold mornings the stove would be lit at least an hour before the service. Mother designed the floor plan for the new rectory that was built in 1935 behind the Presbyterian Church. My grandmother Gilbert taught Sunday school, and mother would drive out to the country to bring in children to Sunday school.

Some of Daddy's bigger jobs were putting in the plumbing and electricity at the Rainwater mansion on Little Yellow and the Hanckle-Nourse House on Big Bear Pen with his ever-ready helper "Sarge" Gibson. That was the same year Docky died. By the early 1940s, my dad had developed a bad back, and Mother and Daddy bought S.T. Marett's real estate and insurance business. Their first office was the downstairs bedroom at the house. Daddy was a great people person, and he took to selling real estate with a flourish, although it wasn't a good time for real estate during the war. But people were still coming up; I don't know where they got the gas ration stamps. Mother handled the property insurance, and she could do that in their office and be at home with Buddy, Sarah and myself. John was just a baby then. Later they rented an office on Main Street.

Grandmother Hall died just a month after Pearl Harbor, and this really hit Daddy hard. She was almost seventy-eight years old and was born while her father, David Norton, was in Virginia near Petersburg, before the Battle of the Crater. Daddy respected his mother for the way she held together and supported the family after T.T died. She had been a strong and resourceful woman, and I believe he inherited a lot of her common sense and ability to make do with what was at hand.

After World War II, the family started going camping on weekends. Mother and Daddy liked it because we children would organize it and get everything together, and Grandmother Gilbert prepared plenty of food. We had a big tent, with room for all of us, including grandmother, and usually we brought some of our friends: Anne Patrick Major (Doggett), Lewis Doggett, Charles Major and Tony were there a lot. Friday afternoon we would go pitch the tent at places like Ammons campground, Satulah Falls Lane or Horse Cove.

As Buddy got older, Daddy would see to it that Bud would have materials to work with. Buddy was always inventing something, and like Daddy he made do with what was around. This usually meant going into Daddy's old shop in the garage next to our house. Even though the plumbing and electrical business had been sold to Curt Wilson, Daddy still kept wire, pipe and other things with which he used to work. A lot of times Mother would ask him to get something at the hardware store, and Daddy would go out to the shop and find what she wanted or sometimes make it out of stuff in the shop. All this came in handy as the needs of the church increased, and they couldn't afford to pay anyone to make, repair or build what was needed. Earlier he had electrified the brass kerosene chandeliers, which are still in use today.

When the Rotary Club was organized in 1946, Daddy was one of the charter members along with Clarence Mitchell and others. He remained a member for a number of years. He also served on the town board of commissioners, the ABC Board and was the first "Realtor at Large" in Highlands in 1951. Later he was charter member of the Highlands Association of the National Board of Real Estate Associations, which became the National Association of Realtors.

Our church had been a mission of the diocese since its inception. When Dr. Herbert Koepp-Baker came to teach at Western Carolina University, Daddy approached him, as he was also an Episcopal priest. He asked Dr. Koepp to serve our church in Highlands. When he accepted, this freed up Dr. A. Rufus Morgan, who was also serving Franklin, Cherokee, Cashiers and several other mission churches in Western North Carolina. Dr. Koepp, as many of us called him, moved with his wife Calista, daughter Suzanne, and son Nicholas into the Church rectory. In just one year, Dr, Koepp suggested to the vestry that they petition to become a parish. He felt that there was enough support from the summer and year-round congregation to make it work. Parish status was granted in 1958. My dad and Dr. Koepp became fast friends, despite my dad's lack of formal education and worldliness. Dr. Koepp recognized Daddy's humility and common sense. They would get into deep discussions about the world, as well as what to do about the furnace.

Sarah and I had married in 1951, and Buddy married the preacher's daughter, Suzanne Koepp-Baker. All of us had left Highlands to live in other parts of the country, but we usually managed to get back on Christmas with our children. Most of the time we stayed with Mother and Daddy, other times with Tony's father. Don't ask how we all managed that. Daddy liked all of his new sons- and daughters-in-law. By 1961, John married Judy Harvey, and they lived in Highlands and worked in the family business. By 1972, when Tony and I moved back to Highlands, Mother was retired and Daddy was senior advisor. Bud and Sue had come back before us by several years. My dad had been on a holiday when the successor of Reverend Gale Webbe, our rector after Dr. Koepp-Baker moved, was selected. Daddy had been senior warden of the church for so long, and he felt he was left out of the search committee process.

Mother had joined a travel club in the '60s. It was "pay now and go later." So they started traveling all over the world: Bermuda, the Hawaiian Islands, Africa, Europe and England. It was in Bermuda that mother got interested in Daddy's family history. His grandfather, Henry Tucker Hall, was born on Bermuda back in 1794, just fourteen years before Daddy's great-grandfather, Rodrick Norton, was born in 1808. A grandfather on one side and a great-grandfather on the other born just fourteen years apart. The Norton family is well documented all the way back to Ireland in the 1600s. But the Hall line doesn't go further back than to Mary D. Hall bringing her two daughters and son, Henry T., to Darien, Georgia, around the first part of the nineteenth century. Mother worked on the Hall ancestry for thirty years, and Tony has picked up the search, with no new findings. Anyway, Mother loved to travel, but I'm not sure Daddy was as keen as she was. I think he liked Highlands and saw no reason to wander.

In the '70s and '80s, she would have one idea after another, and Daddy's favorite expression was, "Marge, you're ruining us." But most of the time things worked out. By the early '70s, Daddy started drawing "welfare"—his name for Social Security. He still went to the office to make sure the boys, Buddy and John, were doing it right. He didn't invent the slogan "service beyond the contract," but he lived by it. Whether it was letting people into their house in the middle of the night because they had left Florida without their key or draining a summer resident's water when an early cold spell threatened frozen and broken pipes, Daddy was a man of his word. In the early '80s, Daddy had a heart attack, and this slowed him down, but not Mother. I believe she thought like a football coach—"Come on Tudor, get up and shake it off."

Family

Daddy died on a cold day in January 1985. It was twenty-five degrees below zero the day he was buried. The family wanted a piper to play at his graveside service. It took something, but his grandson, Scott Paxton, found a piper in Atlanta who agreed to come to Highlands. When we came back to the house after the service, the piper came too and marched back and forth in the front yard for some time before we pleaded for him to come in. Dr. Koepp presided at the church and graveside services. I'll never forget his remembrances of my dad:

> *He was quiet, unassuming and sincere in his contacts with others. He did not appear to cultivate friendships for the advantages that would accrue to himself. To be sure, his personal values prevented him from approving or accepting undesirable motives, qualities or behavior in others. He possessed what local folks characterized as "a kindly way." His vision was at once large but securely based in his home, his family and his community. To some this may have made him provincial in his attitudes and outlook, but he knew where his anchorage lay.*

This is our last article on Highlands history and remembrances. We made a long go of it starting when the Laurel *girls, Marjorie and Janet, first asked us to write* one *article on Highlands history for their publication. That was in May 2002. With just over fifty articles under our belts, it's time to move on, or move out, rather. We have enjoyed remembering the early days, both of my parents' generation and those of the people we knew, and Tony has learned a lot with first biweekly and then monthly deadlines. So thank you all for your kind and appreciative comments about our stories.*

177

BIBLIOGRAPHY

*+Alley, Felix Eugene, Judge. *Random Thoughts and Musings of a Mountaineer.* Salisbury, NC: Rowan Printing Co., 1941.

Alvic, Philis. *Weavers of the Southern Highlands.* Lexington: University Press of Kentucky, 2003.

Balfour, Robert C. *History of St. Thomas Church.* N.p.: self-published, n.d.

*+Buchanan, Carol Jane. *Macon County History II.* Franklin, NC: Norton Weavers, Macon County Historical Society, 1998.

Cathey, James H. *The Genesis of Lincoln.* Kessinger Williams Publishing, 1899, reprinted 2008 by the Confederate Reprint Co. Dahlonega, Georgia.

Family History and Genealogy Records. www.familysearch.org.

Genealogy, Family Trees and Family History Records Online. www.ancestry.com.

*+*History of the First Presbyterian Church: Highlands, North Carolina*. Highlands, NC: self-published, n.d.

*+Hoppen, Dorothee, ed. *The Episcopal Church of the Incarnation: First Hundred Years*. Asheville, NC: Biltmore Press, 1996.

+Laderoute, Linda. *Harlan P. Kelsey Arboretum*.

+Moore, Frank, ed. *Rebellion Record: A Diary of American Events*. Vol. V. New York: G.P Putnam and Sons, 1863.

Moore, Perry. *Stamping Out the Virus: Allied Intervention in the Russian Civil War 1918–1920*. New York: Schiffer Books, 2002.

*+Morgan, Albert Rufus, Reverend. *From Cabin to Cabin*. Murphy, NC: self-published, 1980.

*+———. *History of St. John's Church: Macon County, North Carolina*. Franklin, NC: self-published, 1974.

*+———. *Radiant Light II*. Murphy, NC: self-published, 1974.

*Morgan, Lucy, and Blythe Leggett. *The Gift from the Hills: Carolina*. Raleigh, NC: Bobbs-Merrill, 1958.

*+Parris, John. *Roaming the Mountains*. Asheville, NC: Citizen-Times Publisher, 1955.

*Perrin, Carol Carré. *Highlands Historic Inventory*. Highlands, NC: self-published, 1982.

*Porter, Leona Bryson. *Family of Weimar Siler*. Franklin, NC: self-published, 1951. Publishing committee appointed at the 100th meeting of the Siler family descendants.

Ridpath, John Clarke. *Ridpath's History of the World*. N.p.: Jones Brothers Publishing Co., 1894.

Robb White Papers. McCain Library and Archives, University of Southern Mississippi. *Something About the Author*. Vol. I, 225–26.

RootsWeb. www.rootsweb.com.

*+Shaffner, Randolph. *Heart of the Blue Ridge: Highlands, North Carolina.* Highlands, NC: Faraway Publishing, 2001.

*+Turner, Luther, III. *Macon County History.* Vol. II, *Dr. Charles Frost.* Franklin, NC: Macon County Historical Society, 1998.

*+Watkins, Peggy. *Webbmont.* Highlands, NC: self-published, 1993.

*+Weeks, Charles J., Jr. "An American Naval Diplomat in Revolutionary Russia." Master's thesis, Naval Institute, 1993.

White, Robb, III. "The Most Unforgettable Character I've Met." *Reader's Digest* (July 1953).

+White, Robb, IV. Letters to the authors.

*+Wigginton, Eliot, ed. *Foxfire II.* Rabun Gap-Nacoochee School. New York: Doubleday, 1972.

*Can be found in the Hudson Library
+Authors' library

INDEX

ABOUT THE AUTHORS

Isabel Hall Chambers, a Brenau graduate, is a sixth-generation native of this area and a Norton descendant through her father, Tudor Norton Hall, and grandmother, Meta Norton Frost Hall. Her memories of her family, knowledge of family history and growing up in Highlands are the basis for many of these stories. She  is a founding member and the first president of the Highlands Historical Society. In addition, she was recently appointed historical archivist for the Episcopal Church of the Incarnation. This, along with her interest and knowledge of Highlands's history, has caused her to be sought out by visitors looking up their roots. She is a storyteller and enjoys other storytellers.

Overton "Tony" Chambers was born in Chicago and is Isabel's husband. He came to Highlands with his family in 1936, and a year later they built a summer home in Highlands. At Dartmouth College, he majored in English. He and Isabel and their three sons returned to Highlands in 1972. He is a member of the North Carolina Writer's Network and published his first novel in 2005. His interests are writing, genealogy and history.

Isabel and Tony enjoy researching and writing together.

Also by Overton Chambers:

The Inheritance (2005)